BASIC

ENGLISH GRAMMAR

Third Edition AUDIO CD INCLUDED

Volume A

PEARSON
Longman

Betty Schrampfer Azar
Stacy A. Hagen

Basic English Grammar, Third Edition
Volume A

Azar Associates
Shelley Hartle, Editor
Susan Van Etten, Manager

Pearson Education, 10 Bank Street, White Plains, NY 10606

Editorial manager: Pam Fishman
Project manager: Margo Grant
Development editor: Janet Johnston
Production supervisor: Melissa Leyva
Senior production editor: Robert Ruvo
Director of manufacturing: Patrice Fraccio
Senior manufacturing buyer: Nancy Flaggman
Cover design: Pat Wosczyk
Text composition: Carlisle Communications, Ltd.
Text font: 11/13 Plantin
Illustrations: Don Martinetti

ISBN: 0-13-184939-5

Printed in the United States of America
13 14 15 16–V011–17 16 15 14

CONTENTS

Chapter 8   EXPRESSING PAST TIME, PART 1

Preface to the Third Edition

Basic English Grammar is a beginning level ESL/EFL developmental skills text in which grammar serves as the springboard for expanding learners' abilities in speaking, writing, listening, and reading. It uses a grammar-based approach integrated with communicative methodologies. Starting from a foundation of understanding form and meaning, students engage in meaningful communication about real actions, real things, and their own real lives in the classroom context.

Teaching grammar is the art of helping students look at how the language works and engaging them in activities that enhance language acquisition in all skill areas. The direct teaching of grammar to academically oriented adults and young adults is one component of a well-balanced program of second language instruction and can, much to students' benefit, be integrated into curricula that are otherwise content/context-based or task-based.

This third edition has the same basic approach as earlier editions, with new material throughout. It has

- student-friendly grammar charts with clear information that is easily understood by beginning students.
- numerous exercises to give students lots of practice.
- more illustrations to help students learn vocabulary, understand contexts, and engage in communicative language tasks.
- reorganized chapters with expanded practice for high-frequency structures.
- the option of a student text with or without an answer key in the back.

In addition, the new edition has a greater variety of practice modes, including

- greatly increased speaking practice through extensive use of interactive pair and group work.
- the addition of numerous listening exercises, accompanied by audio CDs, with listening scripts included in the back of the book.
- more activities that provide real communication opportunities.

A new *Workbook* accompanies the student text to provide additional self-study practice. A *Test Bank* is also available.

HOW TO USE THIS TEXT

GRAMMAR CHARTS

The grammar charts present the target structure by way of example and explanation. Teachers can introduce this material in a variety of ways:

a. Present the examples in the chart, perhaps highlighting them on the board. Add additional examples, relating them to students' experience as much as possible. For example, when presenting simple present tense, talk about what students do every day: come to school, study English, etc.

b. Elicit target structures from students by asking questions. (For example, for simple past tense, ask: What did you do last night?) Proceed to selected examples in the chart.

c. Instead of beginning with a chart, begin with the first exercise after the chart, and as you work through it with students, present the information in the chart or refer to examples in the chart.

d. Assign a chart for homework; students bring questions to class. This works best with a more advanced class.

e. Some charts have a preview exercise or pretest. Begin with these, and use them as a guide to decide what areas to focus on. When working through the chart, you can refer to the examples in these exercises.

With all of the above, the explanations on the right side of the chart are most effective when recast by the teacher, not read word for word. Keep the discussion focus on the examples. Students by and large learn from examples and lots of practice, not from explanations. In the charts, the explanations focus attention on what students should be noticing in the examples and the exercises.

FIRST EXERCISE AFTER A CHART

In most cases, this exercise includes an example of each item shown in the chart. Students can do the exercise together as a class, and the teacher can refer to chart examples where necessary. More advanced classes can complete it as homework. The teacher can use this exercise as a guide to see how well students understand the basics of the target structure(s).

SENTENCE PRACTICE

These exercises can be assigned as either oral or written practice, depending on the ability and needs of the class. Many of them can also be done as homework or seatwork.

LET'S TALK

Each "Let's Talk" activity is designated as one of the following: pairwork, small group, class activity, or interview. These exercises encourage students to talk about their ideas, their everyday lives, and the world around them. Examples for each are given so that students can easily transition into the activity, whether it be student- or teacher-led.

LISTENING

Listening exercises for both form and meaning give exposure to and practice with spoken English. Listening scripts for teacher use are in the back of the book. Two audio CDs also accompany the text. Many of the exercises also introduce students to common features of reduced speech.

Teachers may want to play or read aloud some listening scripts one time in their entirety before asking students to write, so they have some familiarity with the overall context. Other exercises can be done sentence by sentence.

WRITING

As students gain confidence in using the target structures, they are encouraged to express their ideas in paragraphs and other writing formats. To help students generate ideas, some of these tasks are combined with "Let's Talk" activities.

When correcting student writing, teachers may want to focus primarily on the structures taught in the chapter.

REVIEW EXERCISES

All chapters finish with review exercises; some are cumulative reviews that include material from previous chapters, so students can incorporate previous grammar with more recently taught structures.

Each chapter review contains an error-correction exercise. Students can practice their editing skills by correcting errors commonly found in beginning students' speaking and writing.

ANSWER KEY

The text is available with or without an answer key in the back. If the answer key is used, homework can be corrected as a class or, if appropriate, students can correct it at home and bring questions to class. In some cases, the teacher may want to collect the assignments written on a separate piece of paper, correct them, and then highlight common problems in class.

For more teaching suggestions and supplementary material, please refer to the accompanying *Teacher's Guide* and visit our teacher-support website, AzarGrammar.com. The website offers free access to

- thousands of worksheets, exercises, games, and activities, all correlated to the Azar texts.
- a discussion forum on teaching grammar.
- *Teacher's Guides* for the *Azar Grammar Series*.
- essays, articles, book reviews, and talks in which Betty Azar shares her thoughts on teaching grammar.
- grammar explanations as presented in the *Azar Interactive* programs.

CHAPTER 1
Using Be

□ **EXERCISE 1. Let's talk: class activity.**

Directions: Ask your classmates their names. Write their first names in the spaces below. You can also ask them what city or country they are from.

FIRST NAME	CITY OR COUNTRY

🎧 *Directions:* Listen to the sentences. Write the words you hear.

Paulo _____*is a student*_____ from Brazil. Marie _____

_____1_____   _____2_____

student from France. _____ the classroom. Today

                              _____3_____

_____ exciting day. _____ the first day of school, but they

_____4_____   _____5_____

_____ nervous. _____ to be here. Mrs. Brown

____6____   _____7_____

_____ the teacher. She _____ in the classroom right now.

___8___   ___9___

_____ late today.

____10____

1-1 NOUN + *IS* + NOUN: SINGULAR

NOUN + *IS* + NOUN
(a) **Canada** **is** a **country**.
	Singular means "one."
	In (a): *Canada* = a singular noun
	        is = a singular verb
	      country = a singular noun

(b) Mexico is **a** country.	**A** frequently comes in front of singular nouns. In (b): **a** comes in front of the singular noun *country*. **A** is called an "article."

(c) **A** cat is **an** animal.	**A** and **an** have the same meaning. They are both articles. **A** is used in front of words that begin with consonants: *b, c, d, f, g, etc.*
	    Examples: *a bed, a cat, a dog, a friend, a girl*
	An is used in front of words that begin with *a, e, i,* and *o*.★
	    Examples: *an animal, an ear, an island, an office*

★*An* is sometimes used in front of words that begin with *u*. See Chart 7-2, p. 183.
Vowels = a, e, i, o, u.
Consonants = b, c, d, f, g, h, j, k, l, m, n, p, q, r, s, t, v, w, x, y, z.

☐ EXERCISE 3. Sentence practice.

Directions: Complete the sentences. Use an article *(a* or *an)*.

1. ____*A*____ horse is ____*an*____ animal.

2. English is _____ language.

3. Tokyo is _____ city.

4. Australia is _____ country.

5. Red is _____ color.

6. _____ dictionary is _____ book.

7. _____ hotel is _____ building.

8. _____ bear is _____ animal.

9. _____ bee is _____ insect.

10. _____ ant is _____ insect.

□ EXERCISE 4. Sentence practice.
Directions: Complete the sentences. Use *a* or *an* and the words in the list.

animal	country	language
city	insect	sport

1. Arabic is ___*a language*___ .

2. Rome is ___*a city*___ .

3. A cat is ___*an animal*___ .

4. Tennis is _____ .

5. Chicago is _____ .

6. Spanish is _____ .

7. Mexico is _____ .

8. A cow is _____ .

9. A fly is _____ .

10. Baseball is _____ .

11. China is _____ .

12. Russian is _____ .

□ EXERCISE 5. Let's talk: small groups.
　　　　Directions: Work in small groups. Choose a leader. Only the leader's book is open.

　　　　Example: a language
　　　　　　LEADER: Name a language.
　　　　SPEAKER A: English is a language.
　　　　SPEAKER B: French is a language.
　　　　SPEAKER C: Arabic is a language.
　　　　　　LEADER: Japanese is a language.
　　　　SPEAKER A: Spanish is a language.
　　　　SPEAKER B: Etc.
　　　　(Continue until no one can name another language.)

　　　　1. an animal　　　　4. a color
　　　　2. a sport　　　　　5. a country
　　　　3. an insect　　　　6. a city

1-2 NOUN + *ARE* + NOUN: PLURAL

NOUN + *ARE* + NOUN (a) **Cats　are　animals.**	*Plural* means "two, three, or more." 　*Cats* = a plural noun 　*are* = a plural verb 　*animals* = a plural noun
(b) SINGULAR: 　a cat, an animal 　　PLURAL: 　　*cats, animals*	Plural nouns end in **-s**. **A** and **an** are used only with singular nouns.
(c) SINGULAR: 　a ci**t*y***, a countr***y*** 　　PLURAL: 　　cit**ies**, countr**ies**	Some singular nouns that end in **-y** have a special plural form: They omit the **-y** and add **-ies**.★
NOUN 　*and* 　NOUN + *ARE* + NOUN (d) **Canada and China 　are countries.** (e) **Dogs　and cats　are animals.**	Two nouns connected by **and** are followed by **are**. In (d): *Canada* is a singular noun. *China* is a singular noun. They are connected by **and**. Together they are plural, i.e., "more than one."

★See Chart 3-6, p. 63, for more information about adding **-s/-es** to words that end in **-y**.

□ EXERCISE 6. Sentence practice.
　　　　Directions: Change the singular sentences to plural sentences.

SINGULAR	PLURAL
1. An ant is an insect. 　→	*Ants are insects.*
2. A computer is a machine. 　→	_____

SINGULAR	PLURAL

3. A dictionary is a book.   → _____

4. A chicken is a bird.   → _____

5. A rose is a flower.   → _____

6. A carrot is a vegetable.   → _____

7. A rabbit is an animal.   → _____

roses

chickens

a rabbit

a carrot

8. Egypt is a country.
   Indonesia is a country.   → _____

9. Winter is a season.
   Summer is a season.   → _____

☐ EXERCISE 7. Game.

Directions: Work in small groups. Close your books for this activity. Your teacher will say the beginning of a sentence. As a group, write the complete sentence. In the end, the group who completes the most sentences correctly wins the game.

Example:
TEACHER *(book open):* Spanish . . . .
GROUP *(books closed):* Spanish is a language.

1. A bear . . . .
2. An ant . . . .
3. London . . . .
4. Spring . . . .
5. A carrot . . . .
6. September and October . . . .
7. Mexico and Canada . . . .
8. A dictionary . . . .
9. Chickens . . . .
10. China . . . .
11. Winter and summer . . . .
12. Arabic . . . .
13. A computer . . . .
14. A fly . . . .

☐ EXERCISE 8. Listening.

Directions: Listen to the sentences. Circle *yes* or *no*.

Example: Cows are animals. (yes)   no
Horses are insects.   yes   (no)

1. yes   no   4. yes   no   7. yes   no

2. yes   no   5. yes   no   8. yes   no

3. yes   no   6. yes   no   9. yes   no

☐ EXERCISE 9. Let's talk: pairwork.

Directions: Your partner will ask you to name something. Answer in a complete sentence. You can look at your book before you speak. When you speak, look at your partner.

Example:

Partner A	Partner B
1. a country	1. two countries
2. an insect	2. a season

PARTNER A: Name a country.
PARTNER B: Brazil is a country.
PARTNER A: Yes, Brazil is a country. Your turn now.

PARTNER B: Name two countries.
PARTNER A: Italy and China are countries.
PARTNER B: Yes, Italy and China are countries. Your turn now.

PARTNER A: Name an insect.
PARTNER B: A bee is an insect.
PARTNER A: Yes, a bee is an insect. Your turn now.

PARTNER B: Name a season.
PARTNER A: Etc.

Remember: You can look at your book before you speak. When you speak, look at your partner.

Partner A	Partner B
1. a language	1. two cities
2. two languages	2. an island
3. a city	3. two countries in Asia
4. an animal	4. a vegetable
5. two seasons	5. a street in this city

1-3 PRONOUN + *BE* + NOUN

	SINGULAR				PLURAL				
	PRONOUN	+ *BE*	+ NOUN		PRONOUN	+ *BE*	+ NOUN		
(a)	*I*	*am*	a student.	(f)	*We*	*are*	students.		
(b)	*You*	*are*	a student.	(g)	*You*	*are*	students.		
(c)	*She*	*is*	a student.	(h)	*They*	*are*	students.		
(d)	*He*	*is*	a student.						
(e)	*It*	*is*	a country.						

I
you
he
she   } = pronouns
it
we
they

am
is   } = forms of *be*
are

(i) Rita is in my class. ***She*** is a student.	Pronouns refer to nouns.
(j) Tom is in my class. ***He*** is a student.	In (i): *she* (feminine) = Rita.
(k) Rita and Tom are in my class. ***They*** are students.	In (j): *he* (masculine) = Tom.
	In (k): *they* = Rita and Tom.

☐ EXERCISE 10. Sentence practice.

Directions: Complete the sentences. Use a verb (***am, is,*** or ***are***). Use a noun
(***a student*** or ***students***).

1. We ___are students___ .   4. Rita and Tom _____ .

2. I _____ .   5. You *(one person)* _____ .

3. Rita _____ .   6. You *(two persons)* _____ .

☐ EXERCISE 11. Let's talk: class activity.

Directions: Close your books. Complete the sentences with *a form of **be*** +
a student/***students***. Point to the student or students as you name them.

Example:
TEACHER: *(name of a student in the class)* Yoko . . . .
STUDENT: *(The student points to Yoko.)* Yoko is a student.

1. *(name of a student)*
2. *(name of a student)* and *(name of a student)*
3. I
4. *(name of a student)* and I
5. We
6. *(name of a student)*
7. *(name of a student)* and *(name of a student)*
8. They
9. You
10. *(name of a student)* and *(name of a student)* and *(name of a student)*

1-4 CONTRACTIONS WITH *BE*

AM	PRONOUN + *BE* → CONTRACTION *I* + *am* → **I'm**	(a) **I'm** a student.
IS	*she* + *is* → **she's** *he* + *is* → **he's** *it* + *is* → **it's**	(b) **She's** a student. (c) **He's** a student. (d) **It's** a city.
ARE	*you* + *are* → **you're** *we* + *are* → **we're** *they* + *are* → **they're**	(e) **You're** a student. (f) **We're** students. (g) **They're** students.

When people speak, they often push two words together. *A contraction =* two words that are pushed together.

Contractions of a *subject pronoun + be* are used in both speaking and writing.

PUNCTUATION: The mark in the middle of a contraction is called an "apostrophe" (').*

*NOTE: Write an apostrophe above the line. Do not write an apostrophe on the line.

CORRECT: _____*I'm a student*_____ .

INCORRECT: _____*I,m a student*_____ .

☐ EXERCISE 12. Sentence practice.

> *Directions:* Complete the sentences. Use contractions *(pronoun + be)*.

1. *Sara* is a student. _____*She's*_____ in my class.

2. *Jim* is a student. _____ in my class.

3. I have *one brother*. _____ twenty years old.

4. I have *two sisters*. _____ students.

5. I have *a dictionary*. _____ on my desk.

6. I like *my classmates*. _____ friendly.

7. I have *three books*. _____ on my desk.

8. *My brother* is twenty-six years old. _____ married.

9. *My sister* is twenty-one years old. _____ single.

10. *Yoko and Ali* are students. _____ in my class.

11. I like *my books*. _____ interesting.

12. I like *grammar*. _____ easy.

13. *Kate and I* live in an apartment. _____ roommates.

14. We live in *an apartment*. _____ on Pine Street.

15. *I* go to school. _____ a student.

16. I know *you*. _____ in my English class.

□ EXERCISE 13. Listening.

👀 *Directions:* Listen to the sentences. Write the contractions you hear. Use the words in the list.

Example:
You will hear: You are in class. You're a student.
You will write: _____ *You're* _____ a student.

I'm	She's	We're
You're	He's	They're
	It's	

1. _____ very nice.

6. _____ in the same class.

2. _____ in the classroom.

7. _____ young.

3. _____ late.

8. _____ very big.

4. _____ a teacher.

9. _____ very friendly.

5. _____ her friend.

10. _____ fun.

□ EXERCISE 14. Listening.

👀 *Directions:* Complete the sentences with the words you hear. Some of them will be contractions.

SPEAKER A: Hello. My name _____ Mrs. Brown.
                        1

                 _____ the new teacher.
                    2

SPEAKER B: Hi. My name _____ Paulo, and
                               3

                 this _____ Marie.
                         4

                 _____ in your class.
                      5

SPEAKER A: _____ nice to meet you.
                    6

SPEAKER B: _____ happy to meet you too.
                       7

SPEAKER A: _____ time for class. Please take a seat.
                    8

1-5 NEGATIVE WITH *BE*

	CONTRACTIONS	*Not* makes a sentence negative.
(a) I *am not* a teacher.	**I'm not**	
(b) You *are not* a teacher.	you**'re not** / you *aren't*	CONTRACTIONS:
(c) She *is not* a teacher.	she**'s not** / she *isn't*	*Be* and *not* can be contracted.
(d) He *is not* a teacher.	he**'s not** / he *isn't*	Note that "I am" has only one
(e) It *is not* a city.	it**'s not** / it *isn't*	contraction with *be*, as in (a), but
(f) We *are not* teachers.	we**'re not** / we *aren't*	there are two contractions with *be*
(g) You *are not* teachers.	you**'re not** / you *aren't*	for (b) through (g).
(h) They *are not* teachers.	they**'re not** / they *aren't*	

□ EXERCISE 15. Sentence practice.

Directions: Write sentences using *is, isn't, are,* and *aren't* and the given information.

Examples: Africa \ city . . . It \ continent
→   *Africa isn't a city. It's a continent.*

Baghdad and Chicago \ city . . . They \ continent
→   *Baghdad and Chicago are cities. They aren't continents.*

1. Canada \ country . . . It \ city

   _____

2. Jakarta \ country . . . It \ city

   _____

3. Beijing and London \ city . . . They \ country

   _____

4. Asia \ country . . . It \ continent

   _____

5. Asia and South America \ continent . . . They \ country

   _____

☐ EXERCISE 16. Sentence practice.

PART I.

Directions: Write the name of the person next to his or her job.

artist _____*Jim*_____   gardener _____

bus driver _____   doctor _____

police officer _____   photographer _____

Jim

Ann

Ms. Black

Mike

Mr. Rice

Sue

PART II.

Directions: Complete the sentences with the correct information.

1. Ann _____*isn't*_____ a gardener. She _*'s a photographer*_____.

2. Mike _____*is*_____ a gardener. He _____ an artist.

3. Jim _____ a bus driver. He _____.

4. Sue _____ a photographer. She _____.

5. Mr. Rice _____ a police officer. He _____.

6. Ms. Black isn't a _____. She _____.

7. I'm not a _____. I'm a _____.

1-6 BE + ADJECTIVE

	NOUN	+	BE	+	ADJECTIVE
(a)	A ball		is		**round.**
(b)	Balls		are		**round.**
(c)	Mary		is		**intelligent.**
(d)	Mary and Tom		are		**intelligent.**
	PRONOUN	+	BE	+	ADJECTIVE
(e)	I		am		**hungry.**
(f)	She		is		**young.**
(g)	They		are		**happy.**

round
intelligent
hungry } = adjectives
young
happy

Adjectives often follow a form of **be** *(am, is, are)*. Adjectives describe or give information about a noun or pronoun that comes at the beginning of a sentence.★

★The noun or pronoun that comes at the beginning of a sentence is called a "subject." See Chart 6-1, p. 158.

☐ EXERCISE 17. Sentence practice.

Directions: Find the adjective in the first sentence. Then complete the second sentence with **be** + *an adjective* that has an opposite meaning. Use the adjectives in the list. Use each adjective only once.

beautiful	expensive	noisy	short
clean	fast	old	tall
easy	✓happy	poor	

1. I'm not sad. I _'m happy_____ .

2. Mr. Thomas isn't rich. He _____ .

3. My hair isn't long. It _____ .

4. My clothes aren't dirty. They _____ .

5. Flowers aren't ugly. They _____ .

6. Cars aren't cheap. They _____ .

7. Airplanes aren't slow. They _____ .

8. Grammar isn't difficult. It _____ .

9. My sister isn't short. She _____ .

10. My grandparents aren't young. They _____ .

11. The classroom isn't quiet. It _____ .

Directions: Write sentences using *is* or *are* and an adjective from the list. Use each adjective only once.

cold	*funny*	*round*	*sweet*
dangerous	✓*hot*	*small/little*	*wet*
dry	*important*	*sour*	
flat	*large/big*	*square*	

1. Fire _____*is hot*_____ .

2. Ice and snow _____ .

3. A box _____ .

4. Balls and oranges _____ .

5. Sugar _____ .

6. An elephant _____ , but a

    mouse _____ .

7. A rain forest _____ , but a

    desert _____ .

8. A joke _____ .

9. Good health _____ .

10. Guns aren't safe. They _____ .

11. A coin _____ small, round, and _____ .

12. A lemon _____ .

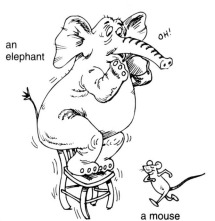

an elephant

OH!

a mouse

a lemon   sugar   water   lemonade

☐ EXERCISE 19. Let's talk: pairwork.

Directions: Complete the drawings by making the faces **happy**, **angry**, **sad**, or **nervous**. Then show your drawings to your partner. Your partner will identify the emotions in your drawings.

 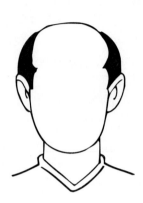 

☐ EXERCISE 20. Sentence practice.

Directions: Complete the sentences. Use *is, isn't, are,* or *aren't*.

1. A ball _____*isn't*_____ square.

2. Balls _____*are*_____ round.

3. Lemons _____ yellow.

bananas

4. Ripe bananas _____ yellow too.

5. A lemon _____ sweet. It _____ sour.

6. My pen _____ heavy. It _____ light.

7. This room _____ dark. It _____ light.

8. My classmates _____ friendly.

9. A turtle _____ slow.

a turtle

10. Airplanes _____ slow. They _____ fast.

11. The floor in the classroom _____ clean. It _____ dirty.

12. The weather _____ cold today.

13. The sun _____ bright today.

14. My shoes _____ comfortable.

☐ **EXERCISE 21. Let's talk: pairwork.**

> *Directions:* Work with a partner. Take turns making two sentences for each picture. Use the given adjectives. You can look at your book before you speak. When you speak, look at your partner.

> *Example:* The girl . . . happy/sad
> PARTNER A: The girl isn't happy. She's sad.
>   Your turn now.

> *Example:* The flower . . . beautiful/ugly
> PARTNER B: The flower is beautiful. It isn't ugly.
>   Your turn now.

Partner A	Partner B
1. The table . . . clean/dirty.	1. The man . . . friendly/unfriendly.
2. The little boy . . . sick/well.	2. The coffee . . . cold/hot.
$x^2 + 5 + 4 = (x + 4)(x + 1)$ 3. The algebra problem . . . easy/difficult.	3. The woman . . . tall/short.
4. The cars . . . old/new.	4. Ken's sister . . . old/young.

□ EXERCISE 22. Let's talk: game.

Directions: Practice using adjectives.

PART I. Look at the words. Check (✓) all the words you know. Your teacher will explain the words you don't know.

1. _____ hungry   11. _____ angry

2. _____ thirsty   12. _____ nervous

3. _____ sleepy   13. _____ quiet

4. _____ tired   14. _____ lazy

5. _____ old   15. _____ hardworking

6. _____ young   16. _____ famous

7. _____ happy   17. _____ sick

8. _____ homesick   18. _____ healthy

9. _____ married   19. _____ friendly

10. _____ single   20. _____ shy

PART II. Sit in a circle. Speaker 1 makes a sentence using **"I"** and the first word. Speaker 2 repeats the information about Speaker 1 and makes a new sentence using the second word. Continue around the circle until everyone in class has spoken. The teacher is the last person to speak and must repeat the information about everyone in the class.

Example:
SPEAKER A: I'm not hungry.
SPEAKER B: He's not hungry.
           I'm thirsty.
SPEAKER C: He's not hungry.
           She's thirsty.
           I'm sleepy.

□ **EXERCISE 23. Let's talk: pairwork.**

Directions: Check (✓) each adjective that describes this city/town (the city or town where you are studying now). When you finish, compare your work with a partner. Do you and your partner have checks beside the same adjectives? Report to the class on things you disagree about.

1. ____ big		11. ____ noisy		
2. ____ small		12. ____ quiet		
3. ____ clean		13. ____ crowded		
4. ____ dirty		14. ____ not crowded		
5. ____ friendly		15. ____ hot		
6. ____ unfriendly		16. ____ cold		
7. ____ safe		17. ____ warm		
8. ____ dangerous		18. ____ cool		
9. ____ beautiful		19. ____ expensive		
10. ____ ugly		20. ____ inexpensive/cheap		

□ **EXERCISE 24. Let's talk: game.**

Directions: Sit in small groups. Close your books for this activity. Your teacher will ask you to name things. As a group, make a list. The teacher will give you only a short time to make the list. Share the list with the rest of your class. The group that makes the longest list gets a point. The group with the most points at the end of the game is the winner.

Example: round
  TEACHER: Name something that is round.
GROUP A's LIST: a ball, an orange, the world
GROUP B's LIST: a baseball, a basketball, a soccer ball
GROUP C's LIST: a ball, a head, an orange, the world, the sun, a planet
Result: Group 3 wins a point.

1. hot	6. flat	11. beautiful
2. square	7. little	12. expensive
3. sweet	8. important	13. cheap
4. sour	9. cold	14. free
5. large	10. funny	15. delicious

1-7 *BE* + A PLACE

(a) Maria is **here**. (b) Bob is **at the library**.	In (a): *here* = a place. In (b): *at the library* = a place. **Be** is often followed by *a place*.
(c) Maria is { **here**. **there**. **downstairs**. **upstairs**. **inside**. **outside**. **downtown**.	A place may be one word, as in the examples in (c).
(d) Bob is { PREPOSITION + NOUN **at** **the library**. **on** **the bus**. **in** **his room**. **at** **work**. **next to** **Maria**.	A place may be a prepositional phrase *(preposition + noun)*, as in (d).

SOME COMMON PREPOSITIONS

above	*between*	*next to*
at	*from*	*on*
behind	*in*	*under*

☐ EXERCISE 25. Sentence practice.

Directions: Complete the sentences with prepositions that describe the pictures. Use each preposition only once.

above	*between*	*next to*	*under*
behind	✓*in*	*on*	

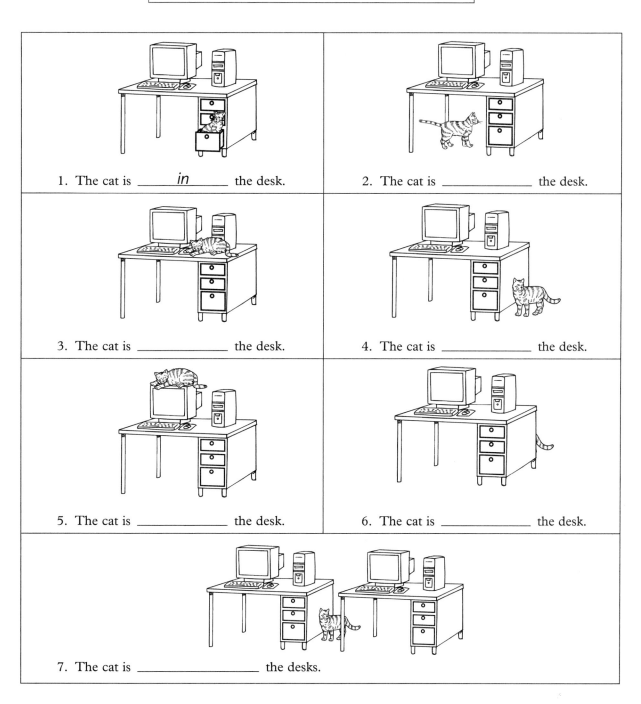

1. The cat is _____*in*_____ the desk.

2. The cat is _____ the desk.

3. The cat is _____ the desk.

4. The cat is _____ the desk.

5. The cat is _____ the desk.

6. The cat is _____ the desk.

7. The cat is _____ the desks.

☐ EXERCISE 26. Let's talk: class activity.

> *Directions:* Close your books. Practice using prepositions of place.

> *Example:* under
> TEACHER: Put your hand under your chair. Where is your hand?
> STUDENT: My hand is under my chair. OR: It's under my chair.

1. on   Put your pen on your book. Where is your pen?
2. in   Put your pen in your book. Where's your pen?
3. under   Put your pen under your book. Where's your pen?
4. next to   Put your pen next to your book. Where's your pen?
5. on   Put your hand on your ear. Where's your hand?
6. next to   Put your hand next to your ear. Where's your hand?
7. above   Put your hand above your head. Where's your hand?
8. next to   Stand next to (. . .). Where are you?
9. between   Stand between (. . .) and (. . .). Where are you?
10. between Put your pen between two books. Where's your pen?
11. behind   Put your hand behind your head. Where's your hand?
12. Follow these directions: Put your pen . . . in your hand.

> . . . on your arm.
> . . . between your hands.
> . . . under your book.
> . . . next to your book.
> . . . above your book.

☐ EXERCISE 27. Let's talk: pairwork.

> *Directions:* Work with a partner. Give and follow directions.
> Partner A: Give directions. Your book is open. You can look at your book before you speak. When you speak, look at your partner.
> Partner B: Draw the pictures Partner A describes. Your book is closed.

> *Example:* Draw a ball on a box.
> PARTNER A *(book open):* Draw a ball on a box.
> PARTNER B *(book closed): (Draw the picture Partner A described.)*

1. Draw a ball on a box.
2. Draw a ball above a box.
3. Draw a ball next to a box.
4. Draw a ball under a box.
5. Draw a ball in a box.
6. Draw a banana between two apples.
7. Draw a house. Draw a bird above the house. Draw a car next to the house. Draw a cat between the car and the house.

8. Draw a flower. Draw a tree next to the flower. Draw a bird above the tree. Draw a turtle under the flower.

Switch roles.
Partner A: Close your book.
Partner B: Open your book. Your turn to talk now.

9. Draw a circle next to a triangle.
10. Draw a circle in a triangle.
11. Draw a circle above a triangle.
12. Draw a triangle between two circles.
13. Draw a circle under a triangle.
14. Draw an apple on a banana. Draw an apple above a banana.
15. Draw a tree. Draw bananas in the trees. Draw a person next to the tree. Draw a dog between the person and the tree.
16. Draw a cloud. Draw a bird under the cloud. Draw a bird above the cloud. Draw a bird in the cloud.

1-8 SUMMARY: BASIC SENTENCE PATTERNS WITH *BE*

(a)	SUBJECT + *BE* + NOUN I am *a student.*	The noun or pronoun that comes at the beginning of a sentence is called the "subject."
(b)	SUBJECT + *BE* + ADJECTIVE He is *intelligent.*	**Be** is a "verb." Almost all English sentences have a subject and a verb.
(c) (d)	SUBJECT + *BE* + A PLACE We are *in class.* She is *upstairs.*	Notice in the examples: There are three basic completions for sentences that begin with a *subject + the verb* **be:** • *a noun,* as in (a) • *an adjective,* as in (b) • *an expression of place,*★ as in (c) and (d)

★An expression of place can be a *preposition + noun,* or it can be one word.

☐ EXERCISE 28. Sentence practice.
Directions: Write the form of **be** *(am, is,* or **are**) that is used in each sentence. Then write the grammar structure that follows **be.**

	BE	+	COMPLETION
1. We're students.	*are*	+	*a noun*
2. Anna is in Rome.	*is*	+	*a place*
3. I'm hungry.	*am*	+	*an adjective*

		BE	+	COMPLETION

4. Dogs are animals. _____ + _____

5. Jack is at home. _____ + _____

6. He's sick. _____ + _____

7. They're artists. _____ + _____

8. I'm in class. _____ + _____

9. Gina is upstairs. _____ + _____

10. Joe's pockets are empty. _____ + _____

☐ EXERCISE 29. Listening.

Directions: **Is** and **are** are often contracted with nouns in spoken English. Listen to the sentences. Practice saying them yourself.

1. Grammar is easy.
   → "Grammar's easy."
2. My name is John.
3. My books are on the table.
4. My brother is 21 years old.
5. The weather is cold today.
6. The windows are open.
7. My money is in my wallet.
8. Mr. Smith is a teacher.
9. Mrs. Lee is at home now.
10. The sun is bright today.
11. Tom is at home right now.
12. My roommates are from Chicago.
13. My sister is a student in high school.

☐ EXERCISE 30. Listening.

Directions: Listen to the sentences. Circle the completions you hear.

Example: My friend _____ from Korea.
   A. is   (B.)'s   C. Ø★

1. The test _____ easy.
   A. is   B. 's   C. Ø

2. My notebook _____ on the table.
   A. is   B. 's   C. Ø

3. My notebooks _____ on the table.
   A. are   B. 're   C. Ø

_____

★ **Ø** = nothing

4. Sue _____ a student.
   A. is   B. 's   C. Ø

5. The weather _____ warm today.
   A. is   B. 's   C. Ø

6. The windows _____ open.
   A. are   B. 're   C. Ø

7. My parents _____ from Cuba.
   A. are   B. 're   C. Ø

8. My cousins _____ from Cuba, too.
   A. are   B. 're   C. Ø

9. My _____ on my desk.
   A. book's   B. books're   C. Ø

10. The _____ in class.
    A. teacher's   B. teachers're   C. Ø

□ EXERCISE 31. Sentence review.

Directions: Complete the sentences. Use *is* or *are*. Then exchange papers and correct each other's sentences.

1. _____ an animal.

2. _____ here.

3. _____ languages.

4. _____ not cheap.

5. _____ friendly.

6. _____ not expensive.

7. _____ an insect.

8. _____ countries.

9. _____ not from Canada.

10. _____ noisy.

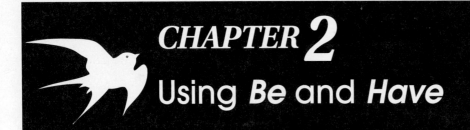

CHAPTER 2
Using *Be* and *Have*

☐ EXERCISE 1. Preview: listening.

Directions: Listen to the questions. Circle *yes* or *no*.

Example: Is Africa a continent? (yes)   no

1. yes	no	4. yes	no	7. yes	no
2. yes	no	5. yes	no	8. yes	no
3. yes	no	6. yes	no	9. yes	no

2-1	YES/NO QUESTIONS WITH *BE*

QUESTION	STATEMENT	In a question, *be* comes in front of the subject.
BE + SUBJECT (a) *Is* *Anna* a student? (b) *Are* *they* at home?	SUBJECT + *BE* *Anna* *is* a student. *They* *are* at home.	PUNCTUATION: A question ends with a question mark (?). A statement ends with a period (.).

☐ EXERCISE 2. Question practice.

Directions: Make questions for the given answers.

1. A: _____*Is Mrs. Lee a teacher?*_____

   B: Yes, Mrs. Lee is a teacher.

2. A: _____

   B: Yes, the sun is a ball of fire.

3. A: _____

   B: Yes, carrots are vegetables.

4. A: _____

   B: Yes, chickens are birds.

5. A: _____

   B: Yes, Mr. Wu is here today.

6. A: _____

   B: Yes, Sue and Mike are here today.

7. A: _____

   B: Yes, English grammar is fun.

8. A: _____

   B: Yes, I am ready for the next grammar chart.

2-2 SHORT ANSWERS TO YES/NO QUESTIONS

QUESTION	SHORT ANSWER	Spoken contractions are not used in short answers that begin with *yes*.
(a) **Is Anna** a student?	→ Yes, **she is**. → No, **she's not**. → No, **she isn't**.	In (a): INCORRECT: *Yes, she's.*
(b) **Are they** at home?	→ Yes, **they are**. → No, **they aren't**.	In (b): INCORRECT: *Yes, they're.*
(c) **Are you** ready?	→ Yes, **I am**. → No, **I'm not**.★	In (c): INCORRECT: *Yes, I'm.*

★*Am* and *not* are not contracted.

□ EXERCISE 3. Question practice.

   Directions: Make questions and give short answers.

1. A: _____*Are you tired?*_____

   B: _____*No, I'm not.*_____ (I'm not tired.)

2. A: _____*Is Anna in your class?*_____

   B: _____*Yes, she is.*_____ (Anna is in my class.)

3. A: _____

   B: _____ (I'm not homesick.)

4. A: _____

   B: _____ (Bob is homesick.)

5. A: _____

   B: _____ (Sue isn't here today.)

6. A: _____

   B: _____ (The students in this class are intelligent.)

7. A: _____

   B: _____ (The chairs in this room aren't comfortable.)

8. A: _____

   B: _____ (I'm not married.)

9. A: _____

   B: _____ (Tom and I are roommates.)

10. A: _____

    B: _____ (A butterfly is not a bird.)

☐ EXERCISE 4. Let's talk: find someone who . . . .

Directions: Walk around the room. Ask your classmates questions. Find someone who can answer *yes* to each question. Write down his/her name. Use ***Are you . . . ?***

Example:
SPEAKER A: Are you hungry?
SPEAKER B: No, I'm not.
SPEAKER A: *(Ask another student.)* Are you hungry?
SPEAKER C: Yes, I am. *(Write down his/her name.)*
         (Now ask another student a different question.)

	First name
1. hungry	
2. sleepy	
3. thirsty	
4. married	
5. a parent	
6. single	
7. happy	

	First name
8. tired	
9. nervous	
10. friendly	
11. lazy	
12. cold	
13. comfortable	
14. from *(name of country)*	

□ EXERCISE 5. Let's talk: pairwork.

Directions: Work with a partner. Ask and answer questions. You can look at your book before you speak. When you speak, look at your partner.

Example: turtles: fast/slow
PARTNER A: Are turtles fast?
PARTNER B: No, they aren't.
PARTNER A: Your turn now.
         OR
PARTNER A: Are turtles slow?
PARTNER B: Yes, they are.
PARTNER A: Your turn now.

Partner A	Partner B
1. a mouse: big/little	1. diamonds: expensive/cheap
2. lemons: sweet/sour	2. your grammar book: light/heavy
3. the world: flat/round	3. butterflies: beautiful/ugly
4. the weather: cool today/warm today	4. English grammar: easy/difficult
5. your dictionary: with you/at home	5. dolphins: intelligent/dumb
6. your shoes: comfortable/uncomfortable	6. the floor in this room: clean/dirty

□ EXERCISE 6. Question practice.

Directions: Complete the conversations with your own words.

1. A: _____*Are*_____ you a student at this school?

    B: Yes, _____.

    A: _____ you from _____?

    B: No, _____ from _____.

2. A: Are you a/an _____?

    B: No, _____ not. I'm a/an _____.

3. A: Are _____ expensive?

    B: Yes, _____.

    A: Is _____ expensive?

    B: No, _____.

4. A: _____ countries in Asia?

   B: Yes, _____ are.

   A: _____ a country in South America?

   B: Yes, _____ is.

   A: _____ a country in Africa?

   B: No, _____ not. It's a country in _____.

2-3   QUESTIONS WITH *BE:* USING *WHERE*

Where asks about place. *Where* comes at the beginning of the question, in front of *be*.

QUESTION	SHORT ANSWER + (LONG ANSWER)
BE + SUBJECT (a) **Is** **the book** on the table? → Yes, *it is*. *(The book is on the table.)* (b) **Are** **the books** on the table? → Yes, *they are*. *(The books are on the table.)*	
WHERE + *BE* + SUBJECT (c) **Where** **is** **the book?** → **On the table.** *(The book is on the table.)* (d) **Where** **are** **the books?** → **On the table.** *(The books are on the table.)*	

□ EXERCISE 7. Question practice.
   Directions: Make questions.

   1. A: _____*Is Kate at home?*_____

      B: Yes, she is. (Kate is at home.)

   2. A: _____*Where is Kate?*_____

      B: At home. (Kate is at home.)

   3. A: _____

      B: Yes, it is. (Cairo is in Egypt.)

   4. A: _____

      B: In Egypt. (Cairo is in Egypt.)

Cairo ★

Nile River

Egypt

5. A: _____

   B: Yes, they are. (The students are in class today.)

6. A: _____

   B: In class. (The students are in class today.)

7. A: _____

   B: On Main Street. (The post office is on Main Street.)

8. A: _____

   B: Yes, it is. (The train station is on Grand Avenue.)

9. A: _____

   B: Over there. (The bus stop is over there.)

10. A: _____

    B: At the zoo. (Sue and Ken are at the zoo today.)

□ EXERCISE 8. Let's talk: pairwork.

Directions: Work with a partner. Ask questions. Use **where**. You can look at your book before you speak. When you speak, look at your partner.

Example:
PARTNER A: Where is your pen?
PARTNER B: It's in my hand. *(or any other true answer)*
PARTNER A: Your turn now.

Partner A	Partner B
1. your dictionary	1. your notebooks
2. your money	2. your wallet
3. your books	3. your glasses or sunglasses
4. your coat	4. your family
5. your pencil	5. your apartment
6. *(name of a classmate)*	6. *(names of two classmates)*
7. your hometown	7. your hometown
8. *(name of a city in the world)*	8. *(name of a country in the world)*

2-4 USING *HAVE* AND *HAS*

SINGULAR	PLURAL	
(a) **I** *have* a pen.	(f) **We** *have* pens.	$\left.\begin{array}{l} I \\ you \\ we \\ they \end{array}\right\}$ **+ have**
(b) **You** *have* a pen.	(g) **You** *have* pens.	
(c) **She** *has* a pen.	(h) **They** *have* pens.	
(d) **He** *has* a pen.		$\left.\begin{array}{l} she \\ he \\ it \end{array}\right\}$ **+ has**
(e) **It** *has* blue ink.		

☐ EXERCISE 9. Sentence practice.

Directions: Complete the sentences. Use **have** and **has**.

1. We ____*have*____ grammar books.

2. I _____ a dictionary.

3. Kate _____ a blue pen. She _____ a blue notebook too.

4. You _____ a pen in your pocket.

5. Bob _____ a notebook on his desk.

6. Anna and Bob _____ notebooks. They _____ pens too.

7. Samir is a student in our class. He _____ a red grammar book.

8. I _____ a grammar book. It _____ a red cover.

9. You and I are students. We _____ books on our desks.

10. Mike _____ a wallet in his pocket. Sara _____ a wallet in her purse.

11. Nadia isn't in class today because she _____ the flu.

12. Mr. and Mrs. Johnson _____ two daughters.

13. Ducks _____ feathers.

14. A duck _____ a beak.

□ EXERCISE 10. Sentence practice.

Directions: Complete the sentences with **have** or **has** and words from the list.

backaches	*a headache*	*a stomachache*
a cold	*a sore throat*	*toothaches*
a fever		

1. Mr. Wu _____.   2. The patients _____.

3. I _____.   4. Mrs. Ramirez _____.   5. You _____.

6. The workers _____.   7. Olga _____.

□ EXERCISE 11. Let's talk: pairwork.

Directions: Complete this conversation with a partner. You can look at your book before you speak. When you speak, look at your partner.

Partner A: How _____?
Partner B: Not so good. _____.
Partner A: That's too bad. Your turn now.

Example:

1. Jim? . . . a toothache
2. Susan? . . . a stomachache

PARTNER A: How's Jim?
PARTNER B: Not so good. He has a toothache.
PARTNER A: That's too bad. Your turn now.

PARTNER B: How's Susan?
PARTNER A: Not so good. She has a stomachache.
PARTNER B: That's too bad. Your turn now.

1. you? . . . a headache
2. you? . . . a sore tooth
3. your mother? . . . a sore back
4. Mr. Lee? . . . a backache

5. your parents? . . . colds
6. the patients? . . . stomachaches
7. your little brother? . . . a sore throat
8. Mrs. Wood? . . . a fever

□ EXERCISE 12. Listening.

Directions: Listen to the sentences. Circle the verbs you hear.

Example: Anna ____ boots. (has) have

ANNA

an earring

a raincoat

a sweater

a button

pants

a zipper

boots

1. has   have
2. has   have
3. has   have
4. has   have
5. has   have
6. has   have
7. has   have
8. has   have

□ EXERCISE 13. Let's talk: find someone who . . . .

Directions: Walk around the room. Ask your classmates questions. Try to find people who can answer *yes* to the questions. Write down their names. Use **Do you have . . . ?**

Example: . . . car?
SPEAKER A: Do you have a car?
SPEAKER B: Yes, I have a car. OR No, I don't have a car.
(You can also give additional information: I have a sports car.)

	First name		First name
1. brothers and sisters?		5. a job?	
2. children?		6. a favorite sport?	
3. pets?		7. a favorite movie star?	
4. hobbies?		8. a favorite movie?	

2-5 USING *MY, YOUR, HIS, HER, OUR, THEIR*

SINGULAR	PLURAL
(a) **I** have a book. **My** book is red.	(e) **We** have books. **Our** books are red.
(b) **You** have a book. **Your** book is red.	(f) **You** have books. **Your** books are red.
(c) **She** has a book. **Her** book is red.	(g) **They** have books. **Their** books are red.
(d) **He** has a book. **His** book is red.	

SUBJECT FORM		POSSESSIVE FORM
I	→	*my*
you	→	*your*
she	→	*her*
he	→	*his*
we	→	*our*
they	→	*their*

I *possess* a book. = I *have* a book. = It is *my* book.

My, our, her, his, our, and *their* are called "possessive adjectives." They come in front of nouns.

□ EXERCISE 14. Sentence practice.

Directions: Complete the sentences with the correct possessive adjectives.

1. You're next. It's _____ turn.

2. Sue's next. It's _____ turn.

3. John and Jane are next. It's _____ turn.

4. My aunt is next. It's _____ turn.

5. I'm next. It's _____ turn.

6. The children are next. It's _____ turn.

7. You and Sam are next. It's _____ turn.

8. Marcos and I are next. It's _____ turn.

9. Bill's next. It's _____ turn.

10. Mrs. Brown is next. It's _____ turn.

□ EXERCISE 15. Sentence practice.

Directions: Complete the sentences with the information on the ID cards.

What information do you know about this person from his ID card?

1. _____ last name is _____.

2. _____ first name is _____.

3. _____ middle initial is _____.

John B. Palmer

What information do the ID
cards give you about Don and
Kathy Johnson?

Don Johnson
10 Broadway
Vista, CA 98301
(888)555-1573

Kathy Johnson
10 Broadway
Vista, CA 98301
(888)555-1573

4. _____ zip code is

_____ .

5. _____ area code is

_____ .

Dr. Diane Ellen Nelson
4/12/70

What do you know about
Dr. Nelson?

6. _____ birthdate is _____ .

7. _____ birthday is _____ .

8. _____ middle name is _____ .

Write about yourself.

9. _____ first name is _____ .

10. _____ last name is _____ .

11. _____ middle name is _____ .

12. _____ middle initial is _____ .

13. _____ area code is _____ .

14. _____ phone number is _____ .

15. _____ zip code is _____ .

☐ **EXERCISE 16. Let's talk: pairwork.**

Directions: Work with a partner. Look at the vocabulary. Put a check (✓) beside the words you know. Ask your partner about the ones you don't know. Your teacher can help you. The pictures below and on the next page illustrate clothing and jewelry.

VOCABULARY CHECKLIST		
Colors	**Clothes**	**Jewelry**
__ black __ blue, dark blue, light blue __ blue green __ brown, dark brown, light brown __ gold __ gray, dark gray, light gray __ green, dark green, light green __ orange __ pink __ purple __ red __ silver __ tan, beige __ white __ yellow	__ belt __ blouse __ boots __ coat __ dress __ gloves __ hat __ jacket __ jeans __ pants __ sandals __ shirt __ shoes __ skirt __ socks __ suit __ sweater __ tie, necktie __ T-shirt	__ bracelet __ earrings __ necklace __ ring __ watch/wristwatch

a hard hat
a T-shirt
an ax(e)
a jacket
a belt
gloves
jeans
boots

an earring
a blouse
a sweater
a ring
a skirt
sandals

☐ **EXERCISE 17.** Sentence practice.

    Directions: Complete the sentences with ***my, your, her, his, our,*** or ***their.***

1. Rita is wearing a blouse. _____*Her*_____ blouse is light blue.

2. Tom is wearing a shirt. _____ shirt is yellow and brown.

3. I am wearing jeans. _____ jeans are blue.

4. Bob and Tom are wearing boots. _____ boots are brown.

5. Sue and you are wearing dresses. _____ dresses are red.

6. Ann and I are wearing sweaters. _____ sweaters are green.

7. You are wearing shoes. _____ shoes are dark brown.

8. Sue is wearing a skirt. _____ skirt is black.

9. John is wearing a belt. _____ belt is white.

10. Sue and Ann are wearing socks. _____ socks are dark gray.

11. Tom is wearing pants. _____ pants are dark blue.

12. I am wearing earrings. _____ earrings are gold.

☐ EXERCISE 18. Let's talk: class activity.

Directions: Your teacher will ask you questions about people and their clothing. Then describe an article of clothing/jewelry and its color. Use this pattern: *possessive adjective + noun + **is/are** + color.* Close your book for this activity.

Examples:
TEACHER: Look at Ali. Tell me about his shirt. What color is his shirt?
STUDENT: His shirt is blue.

TEACHER: Look at Rosa. What is this?
STUDENT: A sweater.
TEACHER: Tell me about her sweater. What color is it?
STUDENT: Her sweater is red.

TEACHER: Look at me. What am I touching?
STUDENT: Your shoes.
TEACHER: Tell me about the color.
STUDENT: Your shoes are brown.

☐ EXERCISE 19. Sentence practice.

Directions: Complete the sentences. Use **have** or **has**. Use **my, your, her, his, our**, or **their**.

1. I ____*have*____ a book. ____*My*____ book is interesting.

2. Bob _____ a backpack. _____ backpack is green.

3. You _____ a raincoat. _____ raincoat is brown.

4. Kate _____ a raincoat. _____ raincoat is red.

5. Ann and Jim are married. They _____ a baby. _____ baby is six months old.

6. Ken and Sue _____ a daughter. _____ daughter is ten years old.

7. John and I _____ a son. _____ son is seven years old.

8. I _____ a brother. _____ brother is sixteen.

9. We _____ grammar books. _____ grammar books are red.

10. Tom and you _____ backpacks. _____ backpacks are brown.

11. Ann _____ a dictionary. _____ dictionary is red.

12. Mike _____ a car. _____ car is blue.

2-6 USING *THIS* AND *THAT*

(a) I have a book in my hand. ***This book*** is red.	*this* book = the book is near me.
(b) I see a book on your desk. ***That book*** is blue.	*that* book = the book is not near me.
(c) ***This*** is my book.	
(d) ***That*** is your book.	
(e) ***That's*** her book.	CONTRACTION: *that is* = *that's*
(f) ***This is*** *("This's")* her book.	In spoken English, *this is* is usually pronounced as "*this's.*" It is not used in writing.

□ EXERCISE 20. Sentence completion.

Directions: Complete the sentences with ***this*** or ***that***.

1. ___*This*___ is my book.	2. ___*That*___ is your book.
3. _____ is a pen.	4. _____ is a pencil.
5. _____ is his notebook.	6. _____ is her notebook.
7. _____ is my dictionary.	8. _____ is your dictionary.
9. _____ is his umbrella.	10. _____ is our umbrella.

□ EXERCISE 21. Let's talk: pairwork.

Directions: Work with a partner. Use ***this*** and ***that***. Touch and point to things in the classroom.

Example: red \ yellow
PARTNER A *(book open)*: red \ yellow
PARTNER B *(book closed)*: This (book) is red. That (shirt) is yellow.
(Partner B touches a red book and points to a yellow shirt.)

1. red \ blue
2. red \ green
3. red \ yellow
4. blue \ black
5. white \ black
6. orange \ green

Switch roles.
PARTNER A: Close your book.
PARTNER B: Open your book. Your turn to talk now.

7. red \ pink
8. dark blue \ light blue
9. black \ gray
10. gold \ silver
11. dark brown \ tan
12. purple \ red

□ EXERCISE 22. Listening.

Directions: Listen to the sentences. Circle the words you hear.

Example: _____ is my pen. (This) That

1. This   That
2. This   That
3. This   That
4. This   That
5. this   that
6. This   That
7. this   that
8. this   that
9. This   That
10. This   That

2-7 USING *THESE* AND *THOSE*

(a) My books are on my desk. ***These*** are my books.		SINGULAR	PLURAL
(b) Your books are on your desk. ***Those*** are your books.		*this* →	*these*
		that →	*those*

□ EXERCISE 23. Sentence practice.
> *Directions:* Complete the sentences with ***these*** or ***those***.

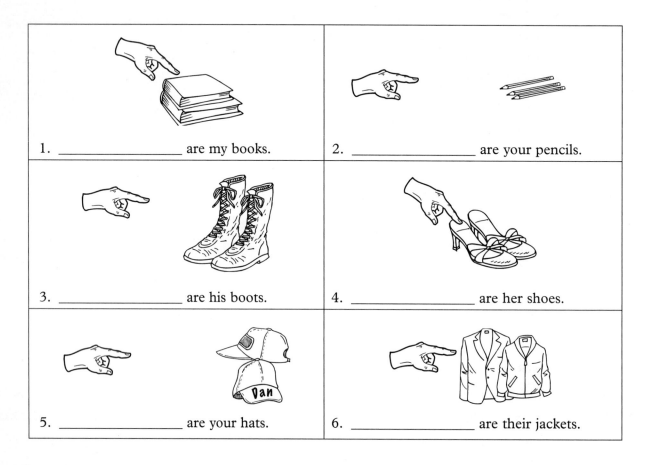

1. _____ are my books.

2. _____ are your pencils.

3. _____ are his boots.

4. _____ are her shoes.

5. _____ are your hats.

6. _____ are their jackets.

□ EXERCISE 24. Sentence practice.
> *Directions:* Complete the sentences. Use the words in parentheses.

1. *(This, These)* _____*These*_____ books belong to me. *(That, Those)*

_____*That*_____ book belongs to Kate.

2. *(This, These)* _____ coat is black. *(That, Those)*

_____ coats are tan.

3. *(This, These)* _____ earrings are gold. *(That, Those)*

_____ earrings are silver.

4. *(This, These)* _____ pencil belongs to Alex.

(That, Those) _____ pencil belongs to Olga.

5. *(This, These)* _____ sunglasses belong to me.

(That, Those) _____ sunglasses belong to you.

6. *(This, These)* _____ exercise is easy. *(That, Those)*

_____ exercises are hard.

7. Students are sitting at *(this, these)* _____ desks, but

(that, those) _____ desks are empty.

8. *(This, These)* _____ book is on my desk. *(That, Those)*

_____ books are on your desk.

□ EXERCISE 25. Let's talk: pairwork.
　　　Directions: Work with a partner. Use **this**, **that**, **these**, or **those**. Touch and point to things in the classroom.

Example:
PARTNER A *(book open):* book
PARTNER B *(book closed):* This is my book. That is your book.

PARTNER A *(book open):* books
PARTNER B *(book closed):* These are my books. Those are your books.

　1. notebook　　　　4. dictionary
　2. coat　　　　　　5. purse
　3. coats　　　　　　6. glasses

Switch roles.
Partner A: Close your book.
Partner B: Open your book. Your turn to talk now.

　7. notebooks　　　10. pens
　8. shoes　　　　　11. pen
　9. wallet　　　　　12. desk

2-8 ASKING QUESTIONS WITH *WHAT* AND *WHO* + *BE*

(a) **What is** this (thing)?	It's a pen.	**What** asks about things.
(b) **Who is** that (man)?	That's Mr. Lee.	**Who** asks about people.
(c) **What are** those (things)?	They're pens.	
(d) **Who are** they?	They're Mr. and Mrs. Lee.	Note: In questions with **what** and **who**,
		• **is** is followed by a singular word.
		• **are** is followed by a plural word.
(e) **What's** this?		CONTRACTIONS
(f) **Who's** that man?		what is = what's
		who is = who's

☐ EXERCISE 26. Sentence practice.

Directions: Complete the questions with **what** or **who** and **is** or **are**.

1. A: _____*Who is*_____ that woman?

   B: She's my sister. Her name is Sonya.

2. A: _____ those things?

   B: They're ballpoint pens.

3. A: _____ that?

   B: That's Ms. Walenski.

4. A: _____ this?

   B: That's my new notebook.

5. A: Look at those people over there. _____ they?

   B: I'm not sure, but I think they're new students from Thailand.

6. A: _____ your name?

   B: Anita.

7. A: _____ your grammar teacher?

   B: Mr. Cook.

8. A: _____ your favorite teachers?

   B: Mr. Cook and Ms. Rosenberg.

9. A: _____ a rabbit?

   B: It's a small furry animal with big ears.

10. A: _____ bats?

    B: They're animals that can fly. They're not birds.

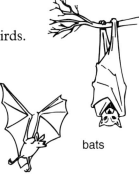

bats

□ EXERCISE 27. Let's talk: pairwork.

Directions: Work with a partner. Talk about things and people in the classroom. You can look at your book before you speak. When you speak, look at your partner.

Example: What's this?
PARTNER A *(book open):* What's this? *(indicating a book)*
PARTNER B *(book closed):* This is your grammar book.

PARTNER A *(book open):* Who's that? *(indicating a classmate)*
PARTNER B *(book closed):* That's Ivan.

1. What's this?
2. Who's that?
3. What's that?
4. What are these?
5. Who's this?
6. What are those?

Switch roles.
PARTNER A: Close your book.
PARTNER B: Open your book. Your turn to ask questions. Use new people and things in your questions.

7. Who's this?
8. What's this?
9. What are those?
10. What's that?
11. Who's that?
12. What are these?

☐ EXERCISE 28. Let's talk: pairwork.

Directions: Work with a partner.

PART I. Write the names of the parts of the body on the illustration. Use the words in the list.

ankle	ear	foot	leg	shoulder
arm	elbow	hand	mouth	side
back	eye	head	neck	teeth
chest	fingers	knee	nose	toes

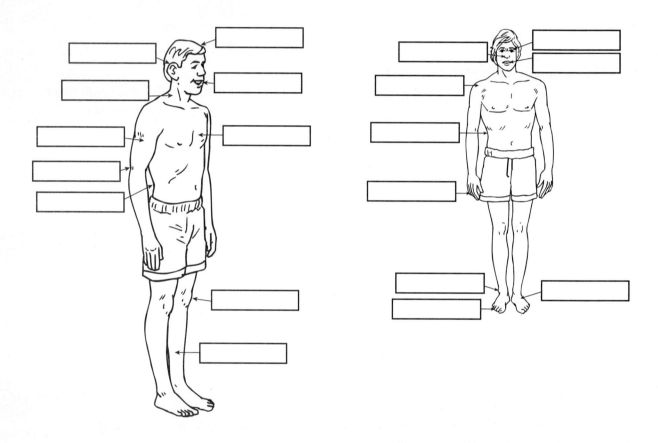

PART II. With your partner, take turns asking questions with ***this, that, these,*** and ***those.***

Note: Both partners can ask about both pictures.

Example:

PARTNER A: What is this?

PARTNER B: This is his leg.

PARTNER B: What are those?

PARTNER A: Those are his fingers.

☐ **EXERCISE 29. Let's talk: class activity.**

Directions: Close your books for this activity. Your teacher will ask questions. **Answer with *this*, *that*, *these*, and *those*.**

Example: hand
TEACHER: What is this? *(The teacher indicates her or his hand.)*
STUDENT: That is your hand.
                OR
TEACHER: What is that? *(The teacher indicates a student's hand.)*
STUDENT: This is my hand.

1. nose	6. knee
2. eyes	7. foot
3. arm	8. shoulder
4. elbow	9. fingers
5. legs	10. ears

☐ **EXERCISE 30. Let's talk: pairwork.**

Directions: Ask your partner questions about the picture on p. 46. Use ***What's this? What's that? What are these? What are those?***
Partner A: Use the list below to point out items on the picture.
Partner B: Look at the picture on p. 46 and name the items your partner points to.

Example: apples
PARTNER A: What are these? *(pointing to apples in the picture)*
PARTNER B: These are apples.

Example: tree
PARTNER A: What's this? *(touching a tree in the picture)*
PARTNER B: This is a tree.

1. apples	4. ears	7. clouds	10. bat
2. fence	5. apple tree	8. dog	11. trees
3. log	6. cow	9. egg	12. turtle

Switch roles.
Partner B: Use the list to point out items on the picture.
Partner A: Look at the picture on p. 46 and name the items your partner points to.

13. animals	16. bee	19. beehive	22. wings
14. grass	17. fences	20. bird	23. tree
15. birds	18. bees	21. chicken	24. hill

☐ EXERCISE 31. Chapter review: error analysis.
    Directions: Correct the errors.

       are
1. We ~~is~~ students.

2. I no hungry.

3. I am student. He is teacher.

4. Yoko not here. She at school.

5. I'm from Mexico. Where you are from?

6. Roberto he is a student in your class?

7. Those pictures are beautifuls.

8. This is you dictionary. It not my dictionary.

9. Mr. Lee have a brown coat.

10. They are n't here today.

11. This books are expensive.

12. Cuba is a island.

☐ EXERCISE 32. Chapter review.
    Directions: Circle the correct completion.

    Example: Those _____ expensive.
        A. book is   Ⓑ books are   C. books is

1. Ann _____ a grammar book.
    A. have   B. is   C. has

2. This floor _____.
    A. dirty is   B. dirty   C. is dirty

3. _____ yellow.
    A. A banana are   B. A banana is   C. Bananas is

4. BOB: _____ is your apartment?

   ANN: It's on Forest Street.

   A. What   B. Where   C. Who

5. Mike is _____ engineer.

   A. a   B. an   C. on

6. Give this to Ann. It is _____ dictionary.

   A. she   B. an   C. her

7. YOKO: _____ these?

   GINA: My art books. I'm taking an art history course.

   A. What is   B. Who are   C. What are

8. TOM: Are you hungry?

   SUE: Yes, _____.

   A. I'm   B. I'm not   C. I am

9. _____ books are really expensive.

   A. Those   B. They   C. This

10. TINA: _____ that?

   JIM: That's Paul Carter.

   A. Who's   B. What's   C. Where's

11. That is _____.

   A. a mistakes   B. mistakes   C. a mistake

12. PAUL: _____ in your class?

   ERIC: No.

   A. Mr. Kim   B. Is Mr. Kim   C. Mr. Kim is he

□ EXERCISE 33. Chapter review.

   Directions: Complete the sentences with *am, is,* or *are.* Use *not* if necessary.

1. Lemons _____ vegetables.

2. A lemon _____ a kind of fruit.

3. I _____ from the United States.

4. We _____ human beings.

5. Eggs _____ oval.

6. Chickens _____ birds, but bats _____ birds.

7. Salt _____ sweet. Sugar _____ sweet.

8. Soccer _____ a sport.

9. Soccer and basketball _____ sports.

10. Africa _____ a country. It _____ a continent.

☐ EXERCISE 34. Chapter review.
Directions: Complete the conversations.

1. A: Where _____ your book?

   B: Yoko _____ it.

   A: Where _____ your notebooks?

   B: Ali and Roberto _____ my notebooks.

2. A: _____ this?

   B: It _____ picture of my family.

   A: _____ this?

   B: That's _____ father.

   A: _____ they?
   B: My brother and sister.

3. A: What's _____?
   B: I don't know. Ask someone else.

   A: What's _____?

   B: It's _____.

4. A: _____ an animal?
   B: Yes.

   A: _____ animals?
   B: Yes.

   A: _____ an insect?
   B: No, it's not. It's an animal too.

5. A: Where _____?

   B: He's _____.

   A: Where _____?

   B: They're _____.

6. A: _____ turtle?

   B: Just a minute. Let me look in my dictionary. Okay. A turtle is a reptile.

   A: _____ reptile?

   B: _____ animal that has cold blood.

   A: _____ snake a reptile too?

   B: Yes. _____ reptiles too.

☐ EXERCISE 35. Review: pairwork.

   Directions: Work with a partner. Give directions using the given prepositions. You can look at your book. When you speak, look at your partner.

   Example: in
   PARTNER A: Put your pen in your pocket.
   PARTNER B: *(Partner B puts her/his pen in her/his pocket.)*
   PARTNER A: Your turn now.

Partner A	Partner B
1. in	1. in
2. on	2. between
3. above	3. behind
4. under	4. above
5. between	5. on
6. next to	6. next to
7. behind	7. under

☐ **EXERCISE 36. Activity: let's talk.**

Directions: Do one or more of these activities. In each activity, ask ***What's this?***
What's that? What are these? What are those? and any other questions you
want to ask.

ACTIVITY 1. Pairwork.
Use a blank sheet of paper. Draw a simple picture of an outdoor scene: for example,
things you can see in a park, on a city street, in the country, at a marketplace. Show
your picture to a partner and answer questions about it.

Sample drawing:

ACTIVITY 2. Group work.
Volunteers can draw pictures of outdoor scenes on the chalkboard, and the class will
ask questions about the pictures.

ACTIVITY 3. Pairwork or group work.
Bring to class pictures without people in them: postcards, photographs, magazine ads,
etc. Show them to a partner or the class and answer questions about them. Your
teacher will help answer questions about vocabulary.

ACTIVITY 4. Pairwork or group work.
Draw the floor plan of your dream house. Show where the kitchen is, the bedrooms,
etc. Show the drawing to a partner or the class and answer questions about it.

☐ **EXERCISE 37. Chapter review.**

Directions: Complete the sentences in this composition by Carlos.

My name _____*is*_____ Carlos. _____*I am* OR *I'm*_____ from Mexico.
₁   ₂

_____ a student. _____ twenty years old.
    3   4

My family lives in Mexico City. _____ father _____ a
                                          5   6

businessman. _____ fifty-one years old. _____ mother
                 7   8

_____ a housewife. _____ forty-nine years old.
    9   10

I _____ two sisters and one brother. The names of my sisters
          11

_____ Rosa and Patricia. Rosa _____ a teacher.
     12   13

_____ twenty-eight years old. Patricia _____ a student.
      14   15

_____ eighteen years old. The name of _____ brother
      16   17

_____ Pedro. _____ an engineer. He is married. He
     18   19

_____ two children.
     20

I live in a dormitory. _____ a tall building on Pine Street. My address
                              21

_____ 3225 Pine St. I live with my roommate. _____ name is Bob.
      22   23

_____ from Chicago. _____ nineteen years old.
      24   25

I like my classes. _____ interesting. I like _____
                          26   27

classmates. _____ friendly.
                  28

□ EXERCISE 38. Review.

Directions: Write a composition by completing the sentences. (Use your own paper.)
Note: A sentence begins with a capital letter (a big letter), and a sentence ends with a
period (.)*

My name _____. I _____ from _____. _____ a student.

_____ years old.

My family lives in _____. _____ father _____ years old. _____

mother _____ years old.

I have _____ sister(s) and _____ brother(s). The name(s) of my sister(s)

_____. _____ is a/an _____. _____ years old.

(Write about each sister.) The name(s) of my brother(s) _____. _____

is a _____. _____ years old. (Write about each brother.)

I live in (a dormitory, a house, an apartment) _____. My address _____. I

live with _____. _____ name(s) _____.

I like _____ classes. _____ are _____ and _____. I like _____

classmates. They _____.

_____

*In British English, a period is called a "full stop."

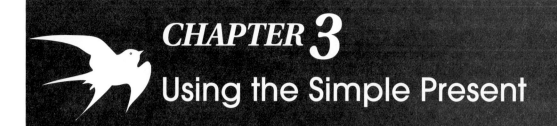

CHAPTER 3
Using the Simple Present

3-1 FORM AND BASIC MEANING OF THE SIMPLE PRESENT TENSE

	SINGULAR	PLURAL	
1st PERSON	**I** *talk*	**we** *talk*	Notice: The verb after **she**, **he**, **it** (3rd person singular) has a final **-s**: *talks*.
2nd PERSON	**you** *talk*	**you** *talk*	
3rd PERSON	**she** *talks*	**they** *talk*	
	he *talks*		
	it *rains*		

(a) I *eat* breakfast **every morning**.	The simple present tense expresses habits.
(b) Olga *speaks* English **every day**.	In (a): Eating breakfast is a habit, a usual
(c) We *sleep* **every night**.	activity. *Every morning* = Monday morning,
(d) They *go* to the beach **every weekend**.	Tuesday morning, Wednesday morning, Thursday morning, Friday morning, Saturday morning, and Sunday morning.

She wakes up every morning at 7:00.

He shaves every morning.

□ EXERCISE 1. Let's talk: pairwork.
　　　　Directions: Work with a partner.

PART I. What do you do every morning? On the left is a list of habits.
Check (✓) your habits every morning. Put them in order. What do you do first,
second, third, etc.? Write them on the lines.

HABITS		MY HABITS EVERY MORNING
_____	eat breakfast	1. *The alarm clock rings.*
_____	go to class	2. ___*I turn off the alarm clock.*___
_____	put on my clothes	3. _____
_____	drink a cup of coffee/tea	4. _____
_____	shave	5. _____
_____	put on my make-up	6. _____
_____	take a shower/bath	7. _____
_____	get up	8. _____
_____	pick up my books	9. _____
_____	walk to the bathroom	10. _____
_____	watch TV	11. _____
_____	look in the mirror	12. _____
___✓___	turn off the alarm clock	13. _____
_____	go to the kitchen/the cafeteria	14. _____
_____	brush/comb my hair	15. _____
_____	say good-bye to my roommate/ wife/husband/parents/partner/etc.	16. _____
_____	brush my teeth	
_____	do exercises	
_____	wash my face	

PART II. Tell a partner about your habits every morning. Close your book.

☐ EXERCISE 2. Listening.

Directions: Listen to the sentences and circle the verbs you hear.

1. (wake)	wakes		6. watch	watches
2. wake	wakes		7. take	takes
3. get	gets		8. take	takes
4. go	goes		9. take	takes
5. do	does		10. talk	talks

☐ EXERCISE 3. Sentence practice.

Directions: Choose the correct completions.

1. My mother and father _____*eat*_____ breakfast at 7:00 every day.
   eat   eats

2. My mother _____ tea with her breakfast.
   drink   drinks

3. I _____ a bath every morning.
   take   takes

4. My sister _____ a shower.
   take   takes

5. I _____ English with my friends.
   study   studies

6. We _____ to school together every morning.
   walk   walks

7. Class _____ at 9:00 every day.
   begin   begins

8. It _____ at 12:00 for lunch.
   stop   stops

9. We _____ in the cafeteria.
   eat   eats

10. My friends and I _____ home at 3:00 every afternoon.
    go   goes

3-2 USING FREQUENCY ADVERBS: *ALWAYS, USUALLY, OFTEN, SOMETIMES, SELDOM, RARELY, NEVER*

100%	*always*	(a) **Bob *always* eats** breakfast.
90%–99%	*usually*	(b) **Mary *usually* eats** breakfast.
75%–90%	*often*	(c) **They *often* watch** TV at night.
25%–75%	*sometimes*	(d) **Tom *sometimes* watches** TV.
5%–10%	*seldom*	(e) **I *seldom* watch** TV.
1%–10%	*rarely*	(f) **I *rarely* drink** milk.
0%	*never*	(g) **I *never* eat** paper.

$$\text{SUBJECT} + \left\{ \begin{array}{l} \textit{always} \\ \textit{usually} \\ \textit{often} \\ \textit{sometimes} \\ \textit{seldom} \\ \textit{rarely} \\ \textit{never} \end{array} \right\} + \text{VERB}$$

The words in this list are called "frequency adverbs." They come between the subject and the simple present verb.★

★Some frequency adverbs can also come at the beginning or at the end of a sentence. For example:
    *Sometimes I get up at seven. I **sometimes** get up at seven. I get up at seven **sometimes**.*
Also: See Chart 3-4, p. 59, for the use of frequency adverbs with *be*.

□ EXERCISE 4. Sentence practice.
    Directions: Complete the sentences in the chart. Use each frequency adverb once.

✓*always*	*often*	*never*	*rarely*	*seldom*	*sometimes*	*usually*

	Sun.	Mon.	Tues.	Wed.	Thurs.	Fri.	Sat.
1. Ann __*always*__ drinks tea with lunch.	☕	☕	☕	☕	☕	☕	☕
2. Bob _____ drinks tea with lunch.		☕	☕	☕	☕	☕	☕
3. Maria _____ drinks tea with lunch.			☕	☕	☕	☕	☕
4. Gary _____ drinks tea with lunch.					☕	☕	☕
5. Ali _____ drinks tea with lunch.						☕	☕
6. Sonya _____ drinks tea with lunch.							☕
7. Joe _____ drinks tea with lunch.							

☐ EXERCISE 5. Sentence practice.

Directions: Write **S** over the subject and **V** over the verb in each sentence. Then rewrite the sentences, adding the *italicized* frequency adverbs.

        S V

1. *always* I eat breakfast in the morning.

        I always eat breakfast   in the morning.

2. *never* I eat carrots for breakfast.

                   for breakfast.

3. *seldom* I watch TV in the morning.

                   in the morning.

4. *sometimes* I have tea with dinner.

                   with dinner.

5. *usually* Sonya eats lunch at the cafeteria.

                   at the cafeteria.

6. *rarely* Joe drinks tea.

7. *often* We listen to music after dinner.

                   after dinner.

8. *always* The students speak English in the classroom.

                   in the classroom.

☐ EXERCISE 6. Let's talk: class activity.

Directions: Your teacher will ask you to talk about your morning, afternoon, and evening activities. Close your books for this activity.

TEACHER: Tell me something you . . .

1. always do in the morning.
2. never do in the morning.
3. sometimes do in the morning.
4. usually do in the afternoon.
5. seldom do in the afternoon.
6. never do in the afternoon.
7. often do in the evening.
8. sometimes do in the evening.
9. rarely do in the evening.
10. sometimes do on weekends.

3-3 OTHER FREQUENCY EXPRESSIONS

(a) I drink tea	once *a day*. twice *a day*. **three times** *a day*. **four times** *a day*. etc.	We can express frequency by saying how many times something happens *a day*. *a week*. *a month*. *a year*.
(b) I see my grandparents **three times** *a week*.		
(c) I see my aunt **once** *a month*.		
(d) I see my cousin Sam **twice** *a year*.		
(e) I see my roommate **every** *morning*. I pay my bills **every** *month*. I see my doctor **every** *year*.		*Every* is singular. The noun that follows (e.g., *morning*) must be singular. *INCORRECT: every mornings*

☐ EXERCISE 7. Sentence practice.

> *Directions:* How often do the people in the chart take the bus? Use the chart to complete the sentences.

	Sun.	Mon.	Tues.	Wed.	Thurs.	Fri.	Sat.
Hamid	🚌	🚌	🚌	🚌	🚌	🚌	🚌
Anna							🚌
Yoko						🚌	🚌
Marco		🚌	🚌	🚌	🚌	🚌	🚌
Joe				🚌	🚌	🚌	🚌
Mr. Wu							
Mrs. Cook					🚌	🚌	🚌

1. Hamid takes the bus _____*seven times*_____ a week. That means he

   _____*always*_____ takes the bus.

2. Anna takes the bus _____ a week. That means she

   _____ takes the bus.

3. Yoko takes the bus _____ a week. That means she

   _____ takes the bus.

4. Marco takes the bus _____ a week. That means he

_____ takes the bus.

5. Joe takes the bus _____ a week. That means he

_____ takes the bus.

6. Mr. Wu _____ takes the bus.

7. Mrs. Cook takes the bus _____ a week. That means she

_____ takes the bus.

☐ **EXERCISE 8. Listening.**

Directions: Listen to the sentences and circle the words you hear.

1. (morning)	mornings	5.	day	days
2. year	years	6.	time	times
3. year	years	7.	night	nights
4. day	days	8.	month	months

3-4 USING FREQUENCY ADVERBS WITH *BE*

SUBJECT + *BE* + FREQUENCY ADVERB	Frequency adverbs follow *am, is, are* (the simple forms of *be*).
Tom + *is* + { *always* *usually* *often* *sometimes* *seldom* *rarely* *never* } + late for class.	
SUBJECT + FREQUENCY ADVERB + OTHER SIMPLE PRESENT VERBS	Frequency adverbs come before all simple present verbs except *be*.
Tom + { *always* *usually* *often* *sometimes* *seldom* *rarely* *never* } + *comes* late.	

☐ EXERCISE 9. Sentence practice.
Directions: Add the frequency adverbs to the sentences.

1. *always*   Ann is on time for class. → *Ann is always on time for class.*
2. *always*   Ann comes to class on time. → *Ann always comes to class on time.*
3. *often*   Maria is late for class.
4. *often*   Maria comes to class late.
5. *never*   It snows in my hometown.
6. *never*   It is very cold in my hometown.
7. *usually*   Bob is at home in the evening.
8. *usually*   Bob stays at home in the evening.
9. *seldom*   Tom studies at the library in the evening.
10. *seldom*   His classmates are at the library in the evening.
11. *sometimes*   I skip breakfast.
12. *rarely*   I have time for a big breakfast.
13. *usually*   I am very hungry by lunchtime.
14. *never*   Sue drinks coffee.

☐ EXERCISE 10. Let's talk: class activity.
Directions: Talk about what your classmates do in the evening.

PART I. Check (✓) the boxes to describe your activities after 5:00 P.M.

	always	usually	often	sometimes	seldom	rarely	never
1. eat dinner							
2. go to a movie							
3. go shopping							
4. go swimming							
5. spend time with my friends							
6. be at home							
7. listen to music							
8. watch videos or DVDs							
9. speak English							
10. send e-mails							
11. surf the Internet							
12. drink coffee after 9:00							
13. be in bed at ten o'clock							
14. go to bed late							

PART II. Exchange books with a partner. Your partner will tell the class two things about your evening.

Example: (Carlos) is usually at home. He sometimes sends e-mails.
(Olga) sometimes drinks coffee after 9:00. She usually goes to bed late.

☐ **EXERCISE 11. Paragraph practice.**
Directions: Write about a typical day in your life, from the time you get up in the morning until you go to bed. Use the following words to show the order of your activities: *then, next, at . . . o'clock, after that, later.*

Example: *I usually get up at seven-thirty. I shave, brush my teeth, and take a shower. Then I put on my clothes and go to the student cafeteria for breakfast. After that I go back to my room. I sometimes watch the news on TV. At 8:15, I leave the dormitory. I go to class. My class begins at 8:30. I'm in class from 8:30 to 11:30. After that I eat lunch. I usually have a sandwich and a cup of tea for lunch.* (Continue until you complete your day.)

3-5 SPELLING AND PRONUNCIATION OF FINAL -ES

			SPELLING	PRONUNCIATION	
-sh	(a)	push	→	pushes	push/əz/	Ending of verb: **-sh, -ch, -ss, -x.**
-ch	(b)	teach	→	teaches	teach/əz/	Spelling: add **-es.**
-ss	(c)	kiss	→	kisses	kiss/əz/	Pronunciation: /əz/.
-x	(d)	fix	→	fixes	fix/əz/	

☐ **EXERCISE 12. Sentence practice.**
Directions: Use the verbs in *italics* to complete the sentences.

1. *brush*   Alice _____*brushes*_____ her hair every morning.

2. *teach*   Alex _____ English.

3. *fix*   Jason _____ his breakfast every morning. He makes eggs and toast.

4. *drink*   Sonya _____ tea every afternoon.

5. *watch*   Joon Kee often _____ television at night.

6. *kiss*   Peter always _____ his children goodnight.

7. *wear*   Tina usually _____ jeans to class.

8. *wash*   Eric seldom _____ dishes.

9. *walk*   Jenny _____ her dog twice each day.

10. *stretch,*   When Jack gets up in the morning, he _____ and
    yawn
    _____ .

☐ EXERCISE 13. Listening.

Directions: Listen to the sentences and circle the verbs you hear.

1. teach	(teaches)	6. watch	watches
2. teach	teaches	7. brush	brushes
3. fix	fixes	8. brush	brushes
4. fix	fixes	9. wash	washes
5. watch	watches	10. wash	washes

☐ EXERCISE 14. Verb form practice.

Directions: Complete the sentences. Use the words in the list and add *-s* or *-es*.
Then practice reading the story aloud (with a partner or in small groups).

brush	*get*	*take*	*wash*
cook	✓ *leave*	*turn*	*watch*
fall	*read*	*sit*	

Laura _____*leaves*_____ her office every night at 5:00 and _____ on

a bus to go home. She has a regular schedule every evening. She _____

dinner and then _____ down to eat at 6:00. After she _____

the dishes, she _____ on the TV. She usually _____ the

news and then a movie. At 9:00, she _____ a shower. She always

_____ her teeth after her shower. Then she picks up a book

and _____ in bed for a while. She usually _____ asleep

before 10:00.

3-6 ADDING FINAL -S/-ES TO WORDS THAT END IN -Y

| (a) cry | → | cries | End of verb: | consonant + -y. |
| try | → | tries | Spelling: | change y to i, add -es. |

| (b) pay | → | pays | End of verb: | vowel + -y. |
| enjoy | → | enjoys | Spelling: | add -s. |

☐ EXERCISE 15. Spelling practice.
    Directions: Complete the chart with the correct form of each verb.

1. I try.	He _____.
2. We study.	She _____.
3. They say.	It _____.
4. You worry.	My mother _____.
5. We fly.	A bird _____.
6. I stay awake.	Paul _____ awake.
7. I enjoy games.	Ann _____ games.
8. Students buy books.	My brother _____ books.
9. We pay bills.	Gina _____ bills.
10. I play music. ♪♪	My friend _____ music.

☐ EXERCISE 16. Sentence practice.
    Directions: Use the words in *italics* to complete the sentences.

1. *pay, always*   Boris _____*always pays*_____ his bills on time.

2. *cry, seldom*   Our baby _____ at night.

3. *study*   Paul _____ at the library every day.

4. *stay, usually*   Laura _____ home at night.

5. *fly*   Kunio is a pilot. He _____ a plane.

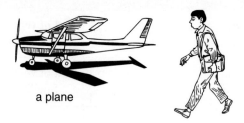

a plane

6. *carry, always*   Carol _____ her books to class.

7. *buy, seldom*   Ann _____ new clothes.

8. *worry*   Tina is a good student, but she _____ about her grades.

9. *enjoy*   Ron _____ good food.

3-7 IRREGULAR SINGULAR VERBS: *HAS, DOES, GOES*

(a) I **have** a book. (b) He **has** a book.	*she* *he* } + **has** /hæz/ *it*	**Have, do,** and **go** have irregular forms for third person singular: *have* → *has* *do* → *does* *go* → *goes*
(c) I **do** my work. (d) She **does** her work.	*she* *he* } + **does** /dəz/ *it*	
(e) They **go** to school. (f) She **goes** to school.	*she* *he* } + **goes** /gowz/ *it*	

☐ EXERCISE 17. Sentence practice.

Directions: Use the given verbs to complete the sentences.

1. *do*   Pierre always ____*does*____ his homework.

2. *do*   We always ____*do*____ our homework.

3. *have*   Yoko and Hamid _____ their books.

4. *have*   Mrs. Chang _____ a car.

5. *go*   Andy _____ to school every day.

6. *have*   Jessica _____ a snack every night around ten.

7. *do*   Sara seldom _____ her homework.

8. *do*   We _____ exercises in class every day.

9. *go, go*   Roberto _____ downtown every weekend. He and his wife

_____ shopping.

10. *go*   My friends often _____ to the beach.

○

□ EXERCISE 18. Listening.

Directions: Listen to the story. Complete the sentences with *is, has, does,* or *goes.*

Marco _____*is*_____ a student. He _____*has*_____ an unusual schedule. All of
           1   2

his classes are at night. His first class _____ at 6:00 P.M. every day. He
                                              3

_____ a break from 7:30 to 8:00. Then he _____ classes from 8:00
        4   5

to 10:00.

He leaves school and _____ home at 10:00. After he _____
                            6   7

dinner, he watches TV. Then he _____ his homework from midnight to 3:00
                                      8

or 4:00 in the morning.

Marco _____ his own computer at home. When he finishes his
          9

homework, he usually goes on the Internet. He usually stays at his computer until the

sun comes up. Then he _____ a few exercises, _____ breakfast, and
                             10   11

_____ to bed. He sleeps all day. Marco thinks his schedule _____
        12   13

great, but his friends think it _____ strange.
                                   14

3-8 SPELLING AND PRONUNCIATION OF FINAL -S/-ES

SPELLING	PRONUNCIATION	
(a) rub → **rubs** ride → **rides** smile → **smiles** dream → **dreams** run → **runs** wear → **wears** drive → **drives** see → **sees** snow → **snows**	rub/z/ ride/z/ smile/z/ dream/z/ run/z/ wear/z/ drive/z/ see/z/ snows/z/	To form a simple present verb in 3rd person singular, you usually add only **-s,** as in (a) and (b). In (a): **-s** is pronounced /z/. The final sounds in (a) are "voiced."★ Voiced sounds make your vocal cords vibrate. The sound /b/ is a voiced sound.
(b) drink → **drinks** sleep → **sleeps** write → **writes** laugh → **laughs**	drink/s/ sleep/s/ write/s/ laugh/s/	In (b): **-s** is pronounced /s/. The final sounds in (b) are "voiceless."★ Your vocal cords do NOT vibrate with voiceless sounds. You push air through your teeth and lips. The sound /p/ is a voiceless sound.
(c) push → **pushes** teach → **teaches** kiss → **kisses** fix → **fixes**	push/əz/ teach/əz/ kiss/əz/ fix/əz/	End of verb: **-sh, -ch, -ss, -x** Spelling: add **-es** Pronunciation: /əz/
(d) cry → **cries** study → **studies**	cry/z/ study/z/	End of verb: consonant + **-y** Spelling: change **y** to **i,** add **-es**
(e) pay → **pays** buy → **buys**	pay/z/ buy/z/	End of verb: vowel + **-y** Spelling: change **y** to **i,** add **-es**
(f) have → **has** go → **goes** do → **does**	/hæz/ /gowz/ /dəz/	The 3rd person singular forms of *have, go,* and *do* are irregular.

★Voiced sounds = b, d, g, l, m, n, r, v, y, and all the vowels: a, e, i, o, u.
Voiceless sounds = f, h, k, p, s, t, th as in *think.*

☐ EXERCISE 19. Let's talk: class activity.

Directions: Talk about everyday activities using the given verbs. Close your book.

Example:
TEACHER: eat
SPEAKER A: I eat breakfast every morning.
TEACHER: What does *(Speaker A)* do every morning?
SPEAKER B: She/He eats breakfast.

1. eat	4. brush	7. get up	10. do	13. put on
2. go	5. have	8. watch	11. listen to	14. carry
3. drink	6. study	9. speak	12. wash	15. kiss

□ EXERCISE 20. Sentence practice.

   Directions: Complete the sentences. Use the words in parentheses. Use the simple present tense. Pay special attention to singular and plural and to the spelling of final *-s/-es*.

1. The students *(ask, often)* ___*often ask*___ questions in class.

2. Pablo *(study, usually)* _____ at the library every evening.

3. Olga *(bite)* _____ her fingernails when she is nervous.

4. Donna *(cash)* _____ a check at the bank once a week.

5. Sometimes I *(worry)* _____ about my grades at school. Sonya *(worry, never)* _____ about her grades. She *(study)* _____ hard.

6. Ms. Jones and Mr. Anderson *(teach)* _____ at the local high school. Ms. Jones *(teach)* _____ math.

7. Birds *(fly)* _____. They *(have)* _____ wings.

8. A bird *(fly)* _____. It *(have)* _____ wings.

9. Jason *(do, always)* _____ his homework. He *(go, never)* _____ to bed until his homework is finished.

10. Mr. Cook *(say, always)*★ _____ hello to his neighbor in the morning.

11. Ms. Chu *(pay, always)*★ _____ attention in class. She *(answer)* _____ questions. She *(listen)* _____ to the teacher. She *(ask)* _____ questions.

_____

★ Pronunciation of **says** = /sɛz/. Pronunciation of **pays** = /peyz/.

12. Sam *(enjoy)* _____ cooking. He *(try, often)* _____

_____ new recipes. He *(like)* _____ to have company for

dinner. He *(invite)* _____ me to dinner once a month. When I

arrive, I *(go)* _____ to the kitchen and *(watch)* _____ him

cook. He usually *(have)* _____

three or four pots on the stove. He *(watch)*

_____ the pots carefully.

He *(make)* _____ a big

mess in the kitchen when he cooks.

After dinner, he *(wash)* _____

all the dishes and *(clean)* _____ the kitchen. I *(cook, never)*

_____. It *(be)* _____ too much trouble. But my

friend Sam *(love)* _____ to cook.

□ EXERCISE 21. Let's talk: pairwork.

Directions: Work with a partner. Use frequency words like **sometimes, rarely,** etc.

PART I. Billy, Jenny, and Peter do many things in their evenings. How often do they do the things in the list? Pay attention to final **-s**.

Example: Billy rarely/seldom does homework.

	BILLY	JENNY	PETER
do homework	once a week	6 days a week	every day
surf the Internet	every day	once a week	once a month
watch TV	3–4 days a week	3–4 days a week	3–4 days a week
read for pleasure	5 days a week	5 days a week	5 days a week
try to go to bed early	once a week	5 nights a week	6 nights a week

PART II. For homework, write ten sentences about the activities of Billy, Jenny, and Peter.

☐ EXERCISE 22. Let's talk and write: pairwork.

Directions: Work with a partner.

Partner A: Tell Partner B five to ten things you do every morning. You can look at the list you made for Exercise 1.

Partner B: Take notes while Partner A is talking. (You will use these notes later to write a paragraph about Partner A's usual morning habits.)

Switch roles.

Partner B: Tell Partner A five to ten things you do every morning.

Partner A: Take notes while Partner B is talking.

When you finish talking, write a paragraph about your partner's daily morning activities. Pay special attention to the use of final *-s/-es*. Show your paragraph to your partner, who will look at your use of final *-s/-es*.

3-9 THE SIMPLE PRESENT: NEGATIVE

(a) **I**	*do not*	drink coffee.	NEGATIVE: $\left.\begin{array}{l} I \\ We \\ You \\ They \end{array}\right\}$ + ***do not*** + *main verb*
We	*do not*	drink coffee.	
You	*do not*	drink coffee.	
They	*do not*	drink coffee.	
(b) **She**	*does not*	drink coffee.	$\left.\begin{array}{l} She \\ He \\ It \end{array}\right\}$ + ***does not*** + *main verb*
He	*does not*	drink coffee.	
It	*does not*	drink coffee.	

Do and ***does*** are called "helping verbs."

Notice in (b): In 3rd person singular, there is no *-s* on the main verb; the final *-s* is part of ***does***.

INCORRECT: She does not drinks coffee.

(c) I ***don't*** drink tea.	CONTRACTIONS: ***do not*** = ***don't***
They ***don't*** have a car.	***does not*** = ***doesn't***
(d) He ***doesn't*** drink tea.	People usually use contractions when they speak.
Mary ***doesn't*** have a car.	People often use contractions when they write.

☐ EXERCISE 23. Sentence practice.

Directions: Use the words in *italics* to make negative sentences. Use contractions.

1. *like, not*   Ingrid ____*doesn't like*____ tea.

2. *like, not*   I ____*don't like*____ tea.

3. *know, not*   Mary and Jim are strangers. Mary _____ Jim.

4. *need, not*   It's a nice day today. You _____

your umbrella.

an umbrella

5. *snow, not*   It _____ in Bangkok in the winter.

6. *speak, not*   I _____ French.

7. *be, not*   I _____ hungry.

8. *live, not*   Butterflies _____ long.

9. *have, not*   A butterfly _____ a long life.

10. *be, not*   A butterfly _____ large.

11. *be, not*   Butterflies _____ large.

a butterfly

12. *have, not*   We _____ class every day.

13. *have, not*   This city _____ nice weather in the summer.

14. *be, not*   It _____ cold today.

15. *rain, not*   It _____ every day.

☐ EXERCISE 24. Let's talk: pairwork.

Directions: Work with a partner. Make two sentences about each picture.

Example:

PARTNER A: Ann takes showers. She doesn't take baths. Your turn now.
PARTNER B: Omar has a dog. He doesn't have a cat. Your turn now.

YES   NO

   1. (Ann \ take)
                                   showers
                                   baths

	YES		NO

2. (Omar \ have)
   a cat
   a dog

3. (I \ drink)
   tea
   coffee

4. (Rob and Ed \ live)
   an apartment
   a house

5. (Becky \ drive)
   a new car
   an old car

6. (I \ play)
   soccer
   tennis

7. (Mr. Davis \ teach)
   English
   French

8. (we \ use)
   typewriters
   computers

9. (Alex \ watch)
   news reports
   old movies

10. (Marco \ study)
    history
    physics

☐ EXERCISE 25. Let's talk: game.

Directions: Sit in a circle. Choose any of the verbs in the list. Make sentences with
not.

| have | like | need | play | read | speak |

Example: like

SPEAKER A: I don't like bananas.
SPEAKER B: *(Speaker A)* doesn't like bananas. I don't have a dog.
SPEAKER C: *(Speaker A)* doesn't like bananas. *(Speaker B)* doesn't have a dog.
I don't play baseball.

Continue around the circle, each time repeating the information of your classmates
before saying your sentence. If you have trouble, your classmates can help you. Your
teacher will be the last one to speak.

☐ EXERCISE 26. Sentence practice.

Directions: Use verbs from the list to complete the sentences. Make all of the
sentences negative by using **does not** or **do not**. You can use contractions
(doesn't/don't). Some verbs may be used more than one time.

do	go	shave
drink	make	smoke
eat	put on	speak

1. Bob _____ *doesn't go* _____ to school every day.

2. My roommates are from Japan. They _____ Spanish.

3. Roberto has a beard. He _____ in the
morning.

4. We _____ to class on Sunday.

5. Sally is healthy. She _____ cigarettes.

6. Jane and Alex always have lunch at home. They _____ at
the cafeteria.

7. Sometimes I _____ my homework in the evening. I watch
TV instead.

8. My sister likes tea, but she _____ coffee.

9. Hamid is a careful writer. He _____ mistakes in spelling when he writes.

10. I'm lazy. I _____ exercises in the morning.

11. Sometimes Ann _____ her shoes when she goes outside.

□ EXERCISE 27. Let's talk: class activity.

Directions: Use the given words to make truthful sentences.

Example: Grass \ blue.
SPEAKER A: Grass isn't blue.
SPEAKER B: Grass is green.

Example: Dogs \ tails.
SPEAKER C: Dogs have tails.
SPEAKER D: People★ don't have tails.

1. A restaurant \ sell shoes.
2. A restaurant \ serve food.
3. People \ wear clothes.
4. Animals \ wear clothes.
5. A child \ need love, food, care, and toys.
6. A child \ need a driver's license.
7. Refrigerators \ hot inside.
8. Refrigerators \ cold inside.
9. A cat \ have whiskers.

10. A bird \ have whiskers.
11. Doctors \ take care of sick people.
12. Doctors in my country \ be expensive.
13. A bus \ carry people from one place to another.
14. It \ be cold today.
15. English \ be an easy language to learn.
16. People in this city \ be friendly.
17. It \ rain a lot in this city.

whiskers

──────────
★*People* is a plural noun. It takes a plural verb.

3-10 THE SIMPLE PRESENT: YES/NO QUESTIONS

	DO/DOES + SUBJECT + MAIN VERB			QUESTION FORMS, SIMPLE PRESENT
(a) **Do**	*I*	*like*	coffee?	
(b) **Do**	*you*	*like*	coffee?	**Do I**
(c) **Do**	*we*	*like*	coffee?	**Do you** + *main verb* (simple form)
(d) **Do**	*they*	*like*	coffee?	**Do we**
				Do they

Does she
Does he + *main verb* (simple form)
Does it

(e) **Does**	*she*	*like*	coffee?	Notice in (e): The main verb in the question does not
(f) **Does**	*he*	*like*	coffee?	have a final **-s**. The final **-s** is part of **does**.
(g) **Does**	*it*	*taste*	good?	INCORRECT: *Does she likes coffee?*

(h) **Are you** a student?	When the main verb is a form of **be**, do is NOT used.
INCORRECT: *Do you be a student?*	See Chart 2-1, p. 24, for question forms with **be**.

QUESTION	SHORT ANSWER	**Do, don't, does**, and **doesn't** are used in the short
		answers to yes/no questions in the simple present.
(i) *Do* you *like* tea? →	Yes, I **do**.	
	No, I **don't**.	
(j) *Does* Bob *like* tea? →	Yes, he **does**.	
	No, he **doesn't**.	

☐ **EXERCISE 28. Question practice.**

Directions: Make questions. Give short answers.

1. A: _____Do you like tea?_____

   B: _____Yes, I do._____ (I like tea.)

2. A: _____Do you like coffee?_____

   B: _____No, I don't._____ (I don't like coffee.)

3. A: _____

   B: _____ (I don't speak Chinese.)

4. A: _____

   B: _____ (Ann speaks Italian.)

5. A: _____

   B: _____ (Ann and Tom don't speak Arabic.)

6. A: _____

   B: _____ (I do exercises every morning.)

7. A: _____

   B: _____ (Sue has a cold.)

8. A: _____

   B: _____ (Jim doesn't do his homework every day.)

9. A: _____

   B: _____ (It rains a lot in April.)

10. A: _____

    B: _____ (Frogs don't have tails.)

□ **EXERCISE 29. Interview and question practice: pairwork.**

Directions: Work with a partner. Ask and answer questions.

PART I. Ask each other about the following activities. Check (✓) the correct box.
You can look at your book before you speak. When you speak, look at your partner.

Example: drive a car
PARTNER A: Do you drive a car?
PARTNER B: No, I don't. Do you drive a car?
PARTNER A: Yes, I do.

	yes	no		yes	no
1. live in an apartment	□	□	6. dream in English	□	□
2. go to movie theaters	□	□	7. have a cell phone	□	□
3. play tennis	□	□	8. like vegetables	□	□
4. enjoy sports on TV	□	□	9. eat red meat	□	□
5. read newspapers every day	□	□	10. like chocolate	□	□

PART II. Write five sentences about your partner. Write five sentences about yourself.

□ **EXERCISE 30. Let's talk: pairwork.**

Directions: Work with a partner. Ask and answer questions.

PART I. Take turns making questions and giving short answers. Use the **names of your classmates** in the questions. Note: This is speaking practice. Do not write the answers yet.

Example:

PARTNER A: _____

PARTNER B: _____ (He is in class today.)

PARTNER A: Is Ali in class today?
PARTNER B: Yes, he is.

Example:

PARTNER B: _____

PARTNER A: _____ (She doesn't speak Spanish.)

PARTNER B: Does Yoko speak Spanish?
PARTNER A: No, she doesn't.

1. Partner A: _____

   Partner B: _____ (He speaks English in class every day.)

2. Partner B: _____

   Partner A: _____ (She comes to class every day.)

3. Partner A: _____

   Partner B: _____ (They're in class today.)

4. Partner B: _____

   Partner A: _____ (She sits in the same seat every day.)

5. Partner A: _____

   Partner B: _____ (He wears jeans every day.)

6. Partner B: _____

   Partner A: _____ (They aren't from Australia.)

7. Partner A: _____

   Partner B: _____ (They don't have dictionaries on

   their desks.)

8. Partner B: _____

   Partner A: _____ (They speak English.)

PART II. Now write the questions and answers in your book.

☐ EXERCISE 31. Let's talk: pairwork.
   Directions: Work with a partner to make conversations. Begin your answers with ***no***.

   Example: children \ walk to school every day
   PARTNER A: Do the children walk to school every day?
   SPEAKER B: No, they don't. They take the bus.
   PARTNER A: Your turn now.

   1. the students \ come to class at 10:00

   2. Amy \ watch TV in the mornings

   3. Luis \ write letters

   4. Beth \ drive a car

   5. the workers \ wear shoes

   6. Joe \ have a cat

students

Amy

Luis

Beth   a worker   Joe

3-11 THE SIMPLE PRESENT: ASKING INFORMATION QUESTIONS WITH *WHERE*

(*WHERE*) + *DO*/ + SUBJECT + MAIN DOES VERB	SHORT ANSWER	(a) = a yes/no question (b) = an information question
(a) **Do** they *live* in Miami? → **Yes,** they do. **No,** they don't.		***Where*** asks for information about a place.
(b) **Where** **do** they *live?* → **In Miami.**		The form of yes/no questions and information questions is the same: ***Do/Does*** + *subject* + *main verb*
(c) **Does** Gina *live* in Rome? → **Yes,** she does. **No,** she doesn't.		
(d) Where **does** Gina *live?* → **In Rome.**		

□ **EXERCISE 32. Question practice.**

Directions: Make questions.

1. A: _____*Does Jean eat lunch at the cafeteria every day?*_____

   B: Yes, she does. (Jean eats lunch at the cafeteria every day.)

2. A: _____*Where does Jean eat lunch every day?*_____

   B: At the cafeteria. (Jean eats lunch at the cafeteria every day.)

3. A: _____

   B: At the post office. (Peter works at the post office.)

4. A: _____

   B: Yes, he does. (Peter works at the post office.)

5. A: _____

   B: Yes, I do. (I live in an apartment.)

6. A: _____

   B: In an apartment. (I live in an apartment.)

7. A: _____

   B: At a restaurant. (Bill eats dinner at a restaurant every day.)

8. A: _____

   B: In the front row. (I sit in the front row during class.)

9. A: _____

   B: At the University of Toronto. (Jessica goes to school at the University of Toronto.)

10. A: _____

    B: On my desk. (My book is on my desk.)

11. A: _____

    B: To class. (I go to class every morning.)

12. A: _____

    B: In class. (The students are in class right now.)

13. A: _____

    B: In Australia. (Kangaroos live in Australia.)

□ EXERCISE 33. Let's talk: pairwork.

   Directions: Work with a partner.
   Partner A: Ask your partner questions using ***where***.
              Your book is open.
   Partner B: Answer the questions. Your book is closed.

   Example: live
   PARTNER A *(book open):* Where do you live?
   PARTNER B *(book closed): (free response)*

   1. live
   2. eat lunch every day
   3. go after class
   4. study at night
   5. go to school
   6. buy school supplies

   Switch roles.
   Partner A: Close your book.
   Partner B: Open your book. Your turn to ask questions now.

   7. buy your clothes
   8. go on weekends
   9. sit during class
   10. eat dinner
   11. do your homework
   12. go on vacation

Q-WORD* + DO/ + SUBJECT + MAIN				SHORT ANSWER	*When* and *what time* ask for information about time.
	DOES		VERB		
(a) **When**	do	you	go	to class? → *At nine o'clock.*	
(b) **What time**	do	you	go	to class? → *At nine o'clock.*	
(c) **When**	does	Anna	eat	dinner? → *At six P.M.*	
(d) **What time**	does	Anna	eat	dinner? → *At six P.M.*	

(e) **What time** do you **usually** go to class?	The frequency adverb usually comes immediately after the subject in a question: *Q-word* + **does**/**do** + subject + **usually** + main verb

*A "Q-Word" is "a question word." *Where, when, what, what time, who,* and *why* are examples of question words.

EXERCISE 34. Question practice.

Directions: Make questions.

1. A: _____*When/What time do you eat breakfast?*_____
   B: At 7:30. (I eat breakfast at 7:30 in the morning.)

2. A: _____*When/What time do you usually eat breakfast?*_____
   B: At 7:00. (I usually eat breakfast at 7:00.)

3. A: _____
   B: At 6:45. (I get up at 6:45.)

4. A: _____
   B: At 6:30. (Maria usually gets up at 6:30.)

5. A: _____
   B: At 8:15. (The movie starts at 8:15.)

6. A: _____
   B: Around 11:00. (I usually go to bed around 11:00.)

7. A: _____
   B: At half-past twelve. (I usually eat lunch at half-past twelve.)

8. A: _____
   B: At 5:30. (The restaurant opens at 5:30.)

9. A: _____

   B: At 9:05. (The train leaves at 9:05.)

10. A: _____

    B: Between 6:30 and 8:00. (I usually eat dinner between 6:30 and 8:00.)

11. A: _____

    B: At eight fifteen. (My classes begin at eight fifteen.)

12. A: _____

    B: At 10:00 P.M. (The library closes at 10:00 P.M. on Saturday.)

□ EXERCISE 35. Let's talk: class interview.

   Directions: Ask and answer questions.

   PART I. Walk around the room. Ask a question using **when** or **what time**. Write
   the answer and your classmate's name. Then ask another classmate a different
   question.

   Example: eat breakfast
   SPEAKER A: When/What time do you eat breakfast?
   SPEAKER B: I usually eat breakfast around seven o'clock.

	Name	Answer
SPEAKER A: *(write)*	*Yoko*	*7 A.M.*

	Name	Answer
1. wake up	_____	_____
2. usually get up	_____	_____
3. eat breakfast	_____	_____
4. leave home in the morning	_____	_____
5. usually get to class	_____	_____
6. eat lunch	_____	_____
7. get home from school	_____	_____
8. have dinner	_____	_____
9. usually study in the evening	_____	_____
10. go to bed	_____	_____

   PART II. Tell the class about a few of the answers you got.

□ EXERCISE 36. Interview and paragraph practice.

Directions: Interview someone (a friend, a roommate, a classmate, etc.) about her/his daily schedule. Use the information from the interview to write a paragraph.

Some questions you might want to ask during the interview:

What do you do every morning?	What time do you . . . ?
What do you do every afternoon?	When do you . . . ?
What do you do every evening?	Where do you . . . ?

3-13 SUMMARY: INFORMATION QUESTIONS WITH *BE* AND *DO*

Q-WORD	+ *BE*	+ SUBJECT		LONG ANSWER
(a) Where	*is*	Thailand?	→	Thailand *is* in Southeast Asia.
(b) Where	*are*	your books?	→	My books *are* on my desk.
(c) When	*is*	the concert?	→	The concert *is* on April 3rd.
(d) What	*is*	your name?	→	My name *is* Yoko.
(e) What time	*is*	it?	→	It *is* ten-thirty.

Q-WORD	+ *DO*	+ SUBJECT	+ MAIN VERB	LONG ANSWER
(f) Where	*do*	you	*live?*	→ I *live* in Los Angeles.
(g) What time	*does*	the plane	*arrive?*	→ The plane *arrives* at six-fifteen.
(h) What	*do*	monkeys	*eat?*	→ Monkeys *eat* fruit, plants, and insects.
(i) When	*does*	Bob	*study?*	→ Bob *studies* in the evenings.

NOTICE: In questions with *be* as the main and only verb, the subject follows *be*. In simple present questions with verbs other than *be,* the subject comes between *do/does* and the main verb.

□ EXERCISE 37. Question practice.

Directions: Complete the questions in the written conversations. Use *is, are, does,* or *do.*

CONVERSATION ONE

A: What time _____*does*_____ the movie start?
        1

B: Seven-fifteen. _____ you want to go with us?
                        2

A: Yes. What time _____ it now?
                    3

B: Almost seven o'clock. _____ you ready to leave?
                            4

A: Yes, let's go.

CONVERSATION TWO

A: Where _____ my keys to the car?
              5

B: I don't know. Where _____ you usually keep them?
                       6

A: In my purse. But they're not there.
B: Are you sure?

A: Yes. _____ you see them?
        7

B: No. _____ they in one of your pockets?
        8

A: I don't think so.

B: _____ your husband have them?
       9

A: No. He has his own set of car keys.
B: Well, I hope you find them.
A: Thanks.

CONVERSATION THREE

A: _____ you go to school?
      10

B: Yes.

A: _____ your brother go to school too?
      11

B: No. He quit school last semester. He has a job now.

A: _____ it a good job?
      12

B: Not really.

A: Where _____ he work?
          13

B: At a restaurant. He washes dishes.

A: _____ he live with you?
      14

B: No, he lives with my parents.

A: _____ your parents unhappy that he quit school?
      15

B: They're very unhappy about it.

A: _____ they want him to return to school?
      16

B: Of course. They have many dreams for him and his future.

□ EXERCISE 38. Let's talk: small group activity.

Directions: Work in small groups. Complete the sentences with *is, are, do,* or *does.*
Circle if the answer is *yes* or *no.* Discuss your answers with your classmates. If you
don't know the answer, guess.

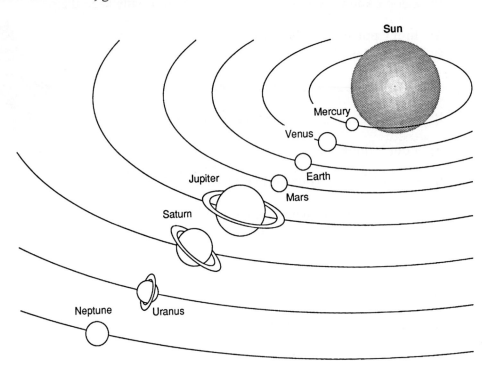

1. ____*Does*____ the moon go around the earth?   (yes)   no

2. _____ the sun go around the earth?   yes   no

3. _____ the planets go around the sun?   yes   no

4. _____ the sun a planet?   yes   no

5. _____ stars planets?   yes   no

6. _____ Venus hot?   yes   no

7. _____ Neptune easy to see?   yes   no

8. _____ Jupiter windy?   yes   no

9. _____ Venus and Mars go around the sun?   yes   no

10. _____ Saturn and Uranus have moons?   yes   no

EXERCISE 39. Question practice.
> *Directions:* Complete the questions and answers with your own words.

1. A: Do _____?
   B: No, I don't.

2. A: Where are _____?
   B: I don't know.

3. A: What time does _____?
   B: _____.

4. A: When do _____?
   B: _____.

5. A: Is _____?
   B: _____.

6. A: What is _____?
   B: _____.

7. A: Are _____?
   B: _____.

8. A: What are _____?
   B: _____.

9. A: What do _____?
   B: _____.

10. A: What does _____?
    B: _____.

□ EXERCISE 40. Chapter review.
> *Directions:* Add **-s** or **-es** where necessary.

ABDUL AND PABLO

s (lives = live + /z/)

(1) My friend Abdul live_∧ in an apartment near school. (2) He walk to school almost every day. (3) Sometimes he catch a bus, especially if it's cold and rainy outside. (4) Abdul share the apartment with Pablo. (5) Pablo come from Venezuela.

(6) Abdul and Pablo go to the same school. (7) They take English classes.

(8) Abdul speak Arabic as his first language, and Pablo speak Spanish. (9) They communicate in English. (10) Sometimes Abdul try to teach Pablo to speak a little Arabic, and Pablo give Abdul Spanish lessons. (11) They laugh a lot during the Arabic and Spanish lessons. (12) Abdul enjoy having Pablo as his roommate, but he miss his family back in Saudi Arabia.

☐ **EXERCISE 41. Chapter review: pairwork.**
Directions: Work with a partner.

PART I.
Partner A: Ask Partner B five questions about things s/he has and doesn't have (for example, a car, a computer, a pet, children, a TV set, a briefcase, etc.). Take notes.
Partner B: Answer the questions.

Example:
PARTNER A: Do you have a car?
PARTNER B: No.
PARTNER A: Do you have a computer?
PARTNER B: Yes, but it's not here. It's in my country.
Etc.

Switch roles. (Partner B now asks five questions.)

PART II.
Partner B: Ask Partner A five questions about things s/he likes and doesn't like (for example, kinds of food and drink, music, movies, books, etc.)
Partner A: Answer the questions.

Example:
PARTNER B: Do you like pizza?
PARTNER A: Yes.
PARTNER B: Do you like the music of *(name of a group or singer)?*
PARTNER A: No, I don't.
Etc.

PART III. Write about your partner. The vocabulary on the next page can help you.
• Give a physical description.
• Write about things this person has and doesn't have.
• Write about things this person likes and doesn't like.

Here's some vocabulary to help you describe your partner.

eye color:
brown
blue
green
gray

hair types:
straight
curly
wavy
bald

hair color:
brown   blond
black   dark
red   light

straight   curly   wavy   bald

☐ EXERCISE 42. Chapter review: question practice.

Directions: Complete the questions and answers with the words in parentheses. Use the simple present of the verbs.

A: *(you, study)* _____ a lot?
                          1

B: I *(study)* _____ at least three hours every night. My roommate
                    2

(study) _____ at least five hours. She's very serious about her
              3

education. How about you? *(you, spend)* _____ a lot of
                                                          4

time studying?

A: No, I don't. I *(spend)* _____ as little time as possible. I
                                    5

(like, not) _____ to study.
                    6

B: Then why *(you, be)* _____ a student?
                                7

A: My parents *(want)* _____ me to go to school. I *(want, not)*
                                8

_____ to be here.
          9

B: In that case, I *(think)* _____ that you should drop out of
                                    10

school and find a job until you decide what you want to do with your life.

☐ EXERCISE 43. Chapter review.

   Directions: Complete each sentence with the correct form of the verb in parentheses.

   I *(have)* _____ two roommates. One of them, Sam, is always neat
   ── 1 ──

and clean. He *(wash)* _____ his clothes once a week. *(you, know)*
                        ── 2 ──

_____ Matt, my other roommate? He *(be)*
          ── 3 ──

_____ the opposite of Sam. For example, Matt *(change, not)*
      ── 4 ──

_____ the sheets on his bed. He *(keep)*
              ── 5 ──

_____ the same sheets week after week. He *(wash, never)*
    ── 6 ──

_____ his clothes. He *(wear)* _____ the same
            ── 7 ──   ── 8 ──

dirty jeans every day. Sam's side of the room *(be, always)* _____
                                                                       ── 9 ──

neat, and Matt's side *(be, always)* _____ a mess. As my mother
                                          ── 10 ──

always *(say)* _____, it *(take)* _____ all kinds of people to
                  ── 11 ──   ── 12 ──

make a world.

Sam's side   Matt's side

☐ EXERCISE 44. Chapter review: let's talk.

   Directions: Work with a partner.

   PART I. Complete the conversations.
   1. PARTNER A: Do you ____?
      PARTNER B: Yes, I do. How about you? Do you ____?
      PARTNER A: ____.

   2. PARTNER B: Are you ____?
      PARTNER A: Yes, I am. How about you? Are you ____?
      PARTNER B: ____.

   3. PARTNER A: ____ you usually ____ in the morning?
      PARTNER B: ____.
      PARTNER A: When ____?
      PARTNER B: ____.

4. PARTNER B: _____?
   PARTNER A: Yes, I do.
   PARTNER B: _____?
   PARTNER A: No, he doesn't.
   PARTNER B: _____?
   PARTNER A: Yes, I am.
   PARTNER B: _____?
   PARTNER A: No, he isn't.

PART II. Share one or two of your dialogues with the class.

□ EXERCISE 45. Chapter review.
   Directions: Make questions. Use your own words.

1. A: _____?
   B: No, I don't.

2. A: _____?
   B: Yes, I am.

3. A: _____?
   B: In an apartment.

4. A: _____?
   B: Six-thirty.

5. A: _____?
   B: Monday.

6. A: _____?
   B: At home.

7. A: _____?
   B: No, he doesn't.

8. A: _____?
   B: No, she isn't.

9. A: _____?
   B: South of the United States.

10. A: _____?
    B: Yes, it is.

11. A: _____?
    B: Yes, they do.

12. A: _____?

    B: In Southeast Asia.

13. A: _____?

    B: Hot in the summer.

14. A: _____?

    B: September.

15. A: _____?

    B: Yes, I do.

☐ EXERCISE 46. Chapter review: let's talk.

Directions: Which lifestyle do you like the most? Ask your teacher questions to get more information about them. Then decide which you like best and explain why.

Example:

SPEAKER A: Where does Peter live?

  TEACHER: On a boat.

SPEAKER B: What does Kathy do?

  TEACHER: She teaches skiing.

SPEAKER C: Where does Ron work?

  TEACHER: At a jewelry store.

SPEAKER D: What pets does Lisa have?

  TEACHER: She has a snake.

Continue asking questions until your chart is complete.

Name	Where does she/he live?	What does he/she do?	Where does she/he work?	What pets does he/she have?
PETER	on a boat			
KATHY		teaches skiing		
RON			at a jewelry store	
LISA				a snake
JACK				

☐ EXERCISE 47. Chapter review: error analysis.

Directions: Correct the errors.

        lives

1. Yoko ~~live~~ in Japan.

2. Ann comes usually to class on time.

3. Peter use his cell phone often.

4. Amy carry a notebook computer to work every day.

5. She enjoy her job.

6. I no know Joe.

7. Mike don't like milk. He never drink it.

8. Tina doesn't speaks Chinese. She speakes Spanish.

9. You a student?

10. Does your roommate sleeps with the window open?

11. A: Do you like strong coffee?

    B: Yes, I like.

12. Where your parents live?

13. What time is your English class begins?

14. Olga isn't need a car. She have a bicycle.

15. Do Pablo does his homework every day?

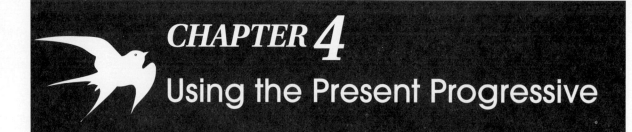

CHAPTER 4
Using the Present Progressive

4-1 *BE + -ING:* THE PRESENT PROGRESSIVE TENSE

am + *-ing*	(a) I **am sitting** in class right now.	In (a): When I say this sentence, I am in class. I am sitting. I am not standing. The action (sitting) is happening right now, and I am saying the sentence at the same time.
is + *-ing*	(b) Rita **is sitting** in class right now.	
are + *-ing*	(c) You **are sitting** in class right now.	
		am, **is**, **are** = helping verbs **sitting** = *the main verb*
		am, is, are + **-ing** = the present progressive tense★

★ The present progressive is also called the "present continuous" or the "continuous present."

☐ EXERCISE 1. Let's talk: class activity.

Directions: Your teacher will perform and describe some actions. Listen for the form of the verb. Answer questions about these actions.

Example: read
TEACHER: *(pantomimes reading)* I am reading. What am I doing?
STUDENT: You are reading.

1. write
2. sit
3. stand
4. count
5. wave
6. look at the ceiling

☐ EXERCISE 2. Let's talk: pairwork.

Directions: Work with a partner. What are the animals in the following pictures doing?
Partner A: Choose any picture and describe the activity. Use the present progressive (*is* + *-ing*).
Partner B: Point to the picture described by your partner.

Example: horse

PARTNER A: The horse is sleeping.

PARTNER B: *(points to the horse in the picture)*

PARTNER A: Your turn now.

Animals		Actions	
bird	mouse	drink a cup of tea	play the piano
cat	horse	drive a car	read a newspaper
dog	monkey	eat a carrot	sleep
elephant	rabbit	sing	take a bath
giraffe	tiger	paint a picture	talk on the phone

□ EXERCISE 3. Let's talk: class activity.

Directions: Answer questions about what you are wearing today and what your classmates are wearing. Use the present progressive (am/is/are + wearing).

Example:
TEACHER: Rosa, what are you wearing today?
SPEAKER A: I'm wearing a white blouse and a blue skirt.
TEACHER: What is Jin Won wearing?
SPEAKER A: He's wearing jeans and a sweatshirt.
TEACHER: What color is his sweatshirt?
SPEAKER A: It's gray with red letters.
TEACHER: What else is Jin Won wearing?
SPEAKER B: He's wearing sneakers, white socks, and a wristwatch.
Etc.

□ EXERCISE 4. Let's talk: pairwork.

Directions: Work with a partner. Identify who is wearing particular articles of clothing. If no one is wearing that piece of clothing, say "no one."

Example:
PARTNER A: brown shoes
PARTNER B: Marco is wearing brown shoes. OR
           Marco and Abdul are wearing brown shoes. OR
           No one is wearing brown shoes.
PARTNER A: Your turn now.

Partner A	Partner B
1. a T-shirt	1. a white shirt
2. blue jeans	2. a skirt (or dress)
3. earrings	3. a necklace
4. boots	4. running shoes
5. pants	5. a belt

□ EXERCISE 5. Let's talk: class activity.

Directions: Act out the directions the teacher gives you. Describe the actions using the present progressive. Continue the action during the description. Close your books for this activity.

Example: Smile.
TEACHER: (Student A), please smile. What are you doing?
SPEAKER A: I'm smiling.

TEACHER: *(Speaker A)* and *(Speaker B)*, please smile. *(Speaker A)*, what are you and *(Speaker B)* doing?

SPEAKER A: We're smiling.

TEACHER: *(Speaker C)*, what are *(Speaker A and Speaker B)* doing?

SPEAKER C: They're smiling.

TEACHER: *(Speaker A)*, please smile. *(Speaker B)*, what is *(Speaker A)* doing?

SPEAKER B: He/She is smiling.

1. Stand up.
2. Sit down.
3. Stand in the middle of the room.
4. Sit in the middle of the room.
5. Stand in the back of the room.
6. Stand between (. . .) and (. . .).
7. Touch the floor.
8. Touch the ceiling.
9. Touch your toes.
10. Open/Close the door/window.
11. Speak in your native language.
12. Shake hands with (. . .).
13. Stand up and turn around in a circle.
14. Hold your book above your head.
15. Hold up your right hand.
16. Hold up your left hand.
17. Touch your right ear with your left hand.
18. Clap your hands.

☐ EXERCISE 6. Let's talk: pairwork.

Directions: Work with a partner. Look around your classroom. Make sentences about people in the room. Use their names. You can use the verbs in the list to help you.

Example: the name of a student near you

PARTNER A: Maria is sitting near me.

PARTNER B: Yes. And she is talking to Po.

PARTNER A: Your turn now.

daydream	*read*	*stand*	*watch*
help	*sit*	*talk*	*wear*
listen	*speak English*	*think in English*	*write*

Partner A	Partner B
1. the name of the teacher	1. the name of a student near the door
2. the names of two classmates near you	2. the names of two classmates on the other side of the room
3. the name of a classmate	3. the names of three classmates
4. yourself *(Use "I.")*	4. yourself and your partner

□ **EXERCISE 7.** Listening.

   Directions: Read the story. Then listen to each sentence and look at the picture of
Tony. Circle the correct answers. Compare your answers with your classmates'
answers.

Tony is not a serious student. He is lazy. He doesn't go to class much. He likes
to sit in the cafeteria. Sometimes he sits alone, and sometimes he visits with friends
from his country. He is in the cafeteria right now. What is he doing?

Example: Tony is talking on his cell phone.   (yes)   no

1. yes	no	6. yes	no
2. yes	no	7. yes	no
3. yes	no	8. yes	no
4. yes	no	9. yes	no
5. yes	no	10. yes	no

□ **EXERCISE 8.** Pretest.

   Directions: Write the **-ing** form for the following words.

1. smile   *smiling*

2. ride   _____

3. run   _____

4. stop   _____

5. rain   _____

6. sleep   _____

7. push   _____

8. count   _____

9. fix   _____   fix

10. write   _____

11. grow   _____

12. wait   _____

4-2 SPELLING OF -ING

	END OF VERB → -ING FORM
Rule 1	A CONSONANT* + -e → DROP THE -e and ADD -ing smile → smiling write → writing
Rule 2	ONE VOWEL* + ONE CONSONANT → DOUBLE THE CONSONANT and ADD -ing** sit → sitting run → running
Rule 3	TWO VOWELS + ONE CONSONANT → ADD -ing; DO NOT DOUBLE THE CONSONANT read → reading rain → raining
Rule 4	TWO CONSONANTS → ADD -ing; DO NOT DOUBLE THE CONSONANT stand → standing push → pushing

*Vowels = a, e, i, o, u.   Consonants = b, c, d, f, g, h, j, k, l, m, n, p, q, r, s, t, v, w, x, y, z.
**Exception to Rule 2: Do not double w, x, and y.   snow → snowing   fix → fixing   say → saying

☐ EXERCISE 9. Spelling practice.
Directions: Write the **-ing** forms for the following words.

1. take ___taking___

2. come _____

3. dream _____

4. bite _____

5. hit _____

6. join _____

7. hurt _____

8. plan _____

9. dine _____

10. snow _____

11. study _____

12. warn _____

□ **EXERCISE 10. Spelling practice.**

Directions: Your teacher will say a sentence. Write the word that ends in **-ing**. Close your book for this activity.

Example: wave
TEACHER: I'm waving.
STUDENTS: *waving*

1. smile
2. fly
3. laugh
4. sit
5. stand
6. sleep
7. clap
8. write

9. eat
10. run
11. sing
12. read
13. drink
14. sneeze
15. cry
16. cut a piece of paper

□ **EXERCISE 11. Let's talk: class activity.**

Directions: Practice using the present progressive to describe actions. Your teacher will give directions. One student acts out the directions, and another describes it.

Example: erase the board
   TEACHER: *(Student A)*, please erase the board.
STUDENT A: *(erases the board)*
   TEACHER: What is *(Student A)* doing?
STUDENT B: He/She is erasing the board.

1. draw a picture on the board
2. clap your hands
3. walk around the room
4. wave at *(name of a student)*
5. sign your name on the board
6. count your fingers out loud
7. hit your desk with your hand
8. carry your book on the top of your head to the front of the room
9. bite your finger
10. look at the ceiling

11. tear a piece of paper
12. sing, hum, or whistle
13. sleep
14. snore
15. stand up and stretch
16. sneeze
17. cough
18. chew gum
19. hold your grammar book between your ankles
20. *(two students)* throw and catch *(something in the room)*

4-3 THE PRESENT PROGRESSIVE: NEGATIVES

(a) I **am not** *sleeping.* I am awake.

(b) Ben **isn't** *listening.* He's daydreaming.

(c) Mr. and Mrs. Brown **aren't** *watching* TV. They're reading.

Present progressive negative:

$$\left.\begin{array}{l} \textbf{am} \\ \textbf{is} \\ \textbf{are} \end{array}\right\} + \textbf{\textit{not}} + \textbf{\textit{-ing}}$$

Ben

Mr. and Mrs. Brown

☐ **EXERCISE 12. Sentence practice.**

Directions: Use the present progressive to make two sentences about each situation, one negative and one affirmative.

Example: Nancy: standing up /sitting down

Written: _____ Nancy isn't standing up. _____

_____ She's sitting down. _____

1.

Otto: watching the news / talking on the phone

Otto isn't _____

He's _____

2.

Anita: listening to music / playing the piano

Anita _____

She's _____

3.

Sophia: reading a magazine / reading a book

Sophia _____

She's _____

4.

The birds: flying / sitting on a telephone wire

The birds _____

They're _____

☐ EXERCISE 13. Let's talk: pairwork.

Directions: Work with a partner. Make sentences about your classmates' activities right now. In the first sentence, describe what is not true. In the second sentence, describe what is true.

Example:

Partner A	Partner B
1. not wearing a white shirt	1. not sitting near us

PARTNER A: Toshi is not wearing a white shirt. He's wearing a blue shirt.
Your turn now.
PARTNER B: Olga is not sitting near us. She's sitting near the teacher. Your turn now.

Partner A	Partner B
1. not standing up	1. not writing
2. not holding a piece of chalk	2. not looking out the window
3. not talking to *(name of a classmate)*	3. not sitting on the floor
4. not wearing T-shirts	4. not standing next to each other *(names of classmates)*

☐ EXERCISE 14. Sentence practice.

Directions: Write the names of people you know. Write two sentences about each person. Write about
(1) what they are doing right now and
(2) what they are not doing right now.
Use your own paper. Share a few of your sentences with the class.

Example: your neighbor
→ *Mrs. Martinez is working at her office right now.*
→ *She is not working in her garden.*

1. someone in your family

2. the leader of your country

3. your favorite actor, writer, or sports star

4. a friend from childhood

QUESTION	→	SHORT ANSWER (+ LONG ANSWER)

	BE + SUBJECT + -ING	
(a)	**Is** Mary **sleeping?**	→ Yes, **she is**. (She's sleeping.)
		→ No, **she's not**. (She's not sleeping.)
		→ No, **she isn't**. (She isn't sleeping.)
(b)	**Are** you **watching** TV?	→ Yes, **I am**. (I'm watching TV.)
		→ No, **I'm not**. (I'm not watching TV.)

	Q-WORD + BE + SUBJECT + -ING	
(c)	**Where** **is** Mary **sleeping?**	→ **In bed.** (She's sleeping in bed.)
(d)	**What** **is** Ted **watching?**	→ **A movie.** (Ted is watching a movie).
(e)	**Why** **are** you **watching** TV?	→ **Because I like this program.** (I'm watching TV because I like this program.)

☐ EXERCISE 15. Question practice.

Directions: Make questions.

1. ____*Is the teacher helping*____ students?

   Yes, she is. (The teacher is helping students.)

2. _____?

   Yes, he is. (John is riding a bicycle.)

3. _____?

   No, I'm not. (I'm not sleeping.)

4. _____ TV?

   No, they aren't. (The students aren't watching TV.)

5. _____ outside?

   No, it isn't. (It isn't raining outside.)

a bicycle

□ **EXERCISE 16. Let's talk: pairwork.**

Directions: Work with a partner. You and your partner have different pictures.
Ask and answer questions about your partner's picture.
Partner A: Look at the pictures in Exercise 2, p. 93.
Partner B: Look at the pictures below. Find the differences.

Example:
PARTNER A: Is the rabbit eating a carrot in your picture?
PARTNER B: No, it isn't. It's eating an ice-cream cone.
PARTNER A: Your turn now.

Partner A	Partner B
1. Is the rabbit . . . ?	1. Is the elephant . . . ?
2. Is the cat . . . ?	2. Is the tiger . . . ?
3. Is the giraffe . . . ?	3. Is the monkey . . . ?
4. Is the horse . . . ?	4. Is the bird . . . ?
5. Is the dog . . . ?	5. Is the mouse . . . ?

□ EXERCISE 17. Let's talk: small groups.
　　　　Directions: Work in small groups. Ask yes/no questions using the present progressive. Use the verbs in the list. Ask two questions for each verb: ***Are you . . . ?*** and ***Is (name of a group member) . . . ?*** Take turns asking questions.

Example: write
SPEAKER A: Are you writing?
SPEAKER B: Yes, I am. OR No, I'm not.
SPEAKER A: Is *(Speaker B)* writing?
SPEAKER C: Yes, she/he is. OR No, she's/he's not.
SPEAKER A: Your turn now, *(Speaker B)*.

1. sit
2. stand
3. smile
4. answer questions
5. sleep

6. speak English
7. look out the window
8. write in your/her/his book
9. talk to *(name of a classmate)*
10. ask me a question

□ EXERCISE 18. Question practice.
　　　　Directions: Create questions with ***where, why,*** and ***what***.

1. A: ___*What are you reading?*___
　　B: My grammar book.　(I'm reading my grammar book.)

2. A: _____
　　B: Because we're doing an exercise.　(I'm reading my grammar book because we're doing an exercise.)

3. A: _____
　　B: A sentence in my grammar book.　(I'm writing a sentence in my grammar book.)

4. A: _____
　　B: In the back of the room.　(Seung is sitting in the back of the room.)

5. A: _____
　　B: In an apartment.　(I'm living in an apartment.)

6. A: _____
　　B: Jeans and a sweatshirt.　(Roberto is wearing jeans and a sweatshirt today.)

7. A: _____
　　B: Because I'm happy.　(I'm smiling because I'm happy.)

☐ EXERCISE 19. Question practice.

Directions: Make questions. Give short answers to yes/no questions.

1. A: What _____*are you writing?*_____

   B: A letter. (I'm writing a letter.)

2. A: _____*Is Ali reading a book?*_____

   B: No, _____*he isn't/he's not.*_____ (Ali isn't reading a book.)

3. A: _____

   B: Yes, _____ (Anna is eating lunch.)

4. A: Where _____

   B: At the Red Bird Cafe. (She's eating lunch at the Red Bird Cafe.)

5. A: _____

   B: No, _____ (Mike isn't drinking a cup of coffee.)

6. A: What _____

   B: A cup of tea. (He's drinking a cup of tea.)

7. A: _____

   B: No, _____ (The girls aren't playing in the street.)

8. A: Where _____
   B: In the park. (They're playing in the park.)

9. A: Why _____
   B: Because they don't have school today. (They're playing in the park because they don't have school today.)

4-5   THE SIMPLE PRESENT vs. THE PRESENT PROGRESSIVE

STATEMENTS (a) I **sit** in class *every day.* (b) I **am sitting** in class *right now.* (c) The teacher **writes** on the board *every day.* (d) The teacher **is writing** on the board *right now.*	• The SIMPLE PRESENT expresses habits or usual activities, as in (a), (c), and (e). • The PRESENT PROGRESSIVE expresses actions that are happening right now, while the speaker is speaking, as in (b), (d), and (f).
QUESTIONS (e) **Do** you **sit** in class every day? (f) **Are** you **sitting** in class right now? (g) **Does** the teacher **write** on the board every day? (h) **Is** the teacher **writing** on the board right now?	• The SIMPLE PRESENT uses **do** and **does** as helping verbs in questions. • The PRESENT PROGRESSIVE uses **am, is,** and **are** in questions.
NEGATIVES (i) I **don't sit** in class every day. (j) I**'m not sitting** in class right now. (k) The teacher **doesn't write** on the board every day. (l) The teacher **isn't writing** on the board right now.	• The SIMPLE PRESENT uses **do** and **does** as helping verbs in negatives. • The PRESENT PROGRESSIVE uses **am, is,** and **are** in negatives.

□ EXERCISE 20. Sentence practice.

Directions: Complete the sentences with the words in parentheses.

1. Ahmed (talk) _____talks_____ to his classmates every day in class. Right now

he (talk) _____ to Yoko. He (talk, not) _____

_____ to his friend Omar right now.

2. It (rain) _____ a lot in this city, but it (rain, not) _____

_____ right now. The sun (shine) _____.

(it, rain) _____ a lot in your hometown?

3. Hans and Anna (sit) _____ next to each other in class every day, so they

often (help) _____ each other with their grammar exercises. Right now

Anna (help) _____ Hans with an exercise on present verb

tenses.

4. Roberto (cook) _____ his own dinner every evening. Right now he is

in his kitchen. He (cook) _____ rice and beans. (he, cook)

_____ meat for his dinner tonight too? No, he is a

vegetarian. He (eat, not) _____ meat. (you, eat) _____

_____ meat? (you, be) _____ a vegetarian?

□ EXERCISE 21. Listening.

Directions: Listen to the sentences. Circle the correct completions.

Examples: John sleeps late . . . .   now   (every day)
          John is sleeping . . . .   (now)   every day

1. now   every day   5. now   every day
2. now   every day   6. now   every day
3. now   every day   7. now   every day
4. now   every day   8. now   every day

☐ **EXERCISE 22. Let's talk: pairwork.**

> *Directions:* Work with a partner. Take turns asking and answering questions about Anna's activities. Use the present progressive and the simple present.

> *Example:* read a newspaper
> PARTNER A: Is Anna reading a newspaper?
> PARTNER B: Yes, she is.
> PARTNER A: Does she read a newspaper every day?
> PARTNER B: Yes, she does.
> PARTNER A: Your turn now.

drink tea	*ride her bicycle*	*talk on the phone*
listen to music	*say "hello" to her neighbor*	*watch TV*
play tennis	*swim*	
play the guitar	*take a walk*	

☐ **EXERCISE 23. Sentence practice.**

> *Directions:* Complete the sentences. Use words from the list.

am	is	are	do	does

1. _____ you ready? The bus _____ leaving right now.

2. _____ you have enough money for the bus?

3. Oh, no. It _____ raining again. _____ it rain often in this city?

4. Excuse me, what time _____ you have?

5. No one is here. _____ I early or late?

6. I _____ looking for the registration office. _____ you know

   where it is?

7. When _____ the registration office close?

8. Where _____ your school?

9. Where _____ you live?

10. _____ your classmates live near you?

□ EXERCISE 24. Question practice.

　　Directions: Complete the sentences with the words in parentheses.

　　1. A: Tom is on the phone.

　　　 B: *(he, talk)* _____*Is he talking*_ to his wife?

　　　 A: Yes.

　　　 B: *(he, talk)* _____*Does he talk*_____ to her often?

　　　 A: Yes, he *(talk)* _____*talks*_____to her every day during his lunch break.

　　2. A: I *(walk)* _____ to school every day. I *(take, not)* _____

　　　　 _____ the bus. *(you, take)* _____ the bus?

　　　 B: No, I don't.

　　3. A: Anna is in the hallway.

　　　 B: *(she, talk)* _____ to her friends?

　　　 A: No, she isn't. She *(run)* _____ to her next class.

　　4. A: I *(read)* _____ the newspaper every day.

　　　 B: How about your grammar book? *(you, read)* _____
　　　　 your grammar book every day?

　　　 A: No, I don't. I *(read, not)* _____ my grammar book
　　　　 every day.

　　5. A: What *(you, read)* _____ right now?

　　　 B: I *(read)* _____ my grammar book.

6. A: *(you, want)* _____ your coat?

   B: Yes.

   A: *(be, this)* _____ your coat?

   B: No, my coat *(hang)* _____ in the closet.

☐ **EXERCISE 25. Listening.**

Directions: Listen to each conversation. Complete the sentences with the words you hear.

Example:

You will hear: Is Ann here today?

You will write: ____*Is*____ Ann here today?

You will hear: No. She's working at her uncle's bakery today.

You will write: No. _____*She's working*_____ at her uncle's bakery today.

1. A: _____ Tom _____ a black hat?

   B: Yes.

   A: _____ it every day?

   B: No.

   A: _____ it right now?

   B: I _____. Why do you care about Tom's hat?

   A: I found a hat in my apartment. Someone left it there. I _____ that it belongs to Tom.

2. A: _____ animals _____?

   B: I don't know. I suppose so. Animals _____ very different from human beings in lots of ways.

   A: Look at my dog. She _____. Her eyes _____ closed. At the same time, she _____ and _____ her head and her front legs. I _____ sure that she _____ right now. I'm sure that animals _____.

☐ **EXERCISE 26. Listening.**

Directions: Listen to the conversation. Complete the sentences with the words you hear.

Example:
You will hear: Are you doing an exercise?
You will write: _____*Are you doing*_____ an exercise?
You will hear: Yes, I am.
You will write: Yes, _____*I am*_____.

SPEAKER A: What are you doing? _____ on your English paper?

SPEAKER B: No, _____. _____ an e-mail to my sister.

SPEAKER A: _____ to her often?

SPEAKER B: Yes, but I _____ a lot of e-mails to anyone else.

SPEAKER A: _____ to you often?

SPEAKER B: Yes. I _____ an e-mail from her several times a week. How about you? _____ a lot of e-mails?

SPEAKER A: Yes. I _____ to send e-mails to friends all over the world.

4-6 NONACTION VERBS NOT USED IN THE PRESENT PROGRESSIVE

(a) I'm hungry *right now*. I *want* an apple. *INCORRECT: I am wanting an apple.* (b) I *hear* a siren. *Do* you *hear* it too? *INCORRECT: I'm hearing a siren. Are you hearing it too?*	Some verbs are NOT used in the present progressive. They are called "nonaction verbs." In (a): *Want* is a nonaction verb. *Want* expresses a physical or emotional need, not an action. In (b): *Hear* is a nonaction verb. *Hear* expresses a sensory experience, not an action.

NONACTION VERBS

dislike	*hear*	*believe*
hate	*see*	*know*
like	*smell*	*think* (meaning *believe*)*
love	*taste*	*understand*
need		
want		

*Sometimes *think* is used in progressive tenses. See Chart 4-8, p. 117, for a discussion of *think about* and *think that*.

□ EXERCISE 27. Sentence practice.
    Directions: Use the words in parentheses to complete the sentences. Use the simple present or the present progressive.

1. Alice is in her room right now. She *(read)* _____*is reading*_____ a book. She *(like)*

    _____*likes*_____ the book.

2. It *(snow)* _____ right now. It's beautiful! I *(like)*

    _____ this weather.

3. I *(know)* _____ Jessica Jones. She's in my class.

4. The teacher *(talk)* _____ to us right now. I *(understand)*

    _____ everything she's saying.

5. Mike is at a restaurant right now. He *(eat)* _____ dinner.

    He *(like)* _____ the food. It *(taste)* _____ good.

6. Sniff-sniff. I *(smell)* _____ gas. *(you, smell)* _____

    _____ it too?

7. Jason *(tell)* _____ us a story right now. I *(believe)*

    _____ his story. I *(think)* _____ that his story is true.

8. Ugh! Someone *(smoke)* _____ a cigar. It *(smell)*

    _____ terrible! I *(hate)* _____ cigars.

9. Look at Mr. Allen. He *(hold)* _____ a kitten in his hand.

    He *(love)* _____ the kitten. Mr. Allen *(smile)*

    _____ .

☐ EXERCISE 28. Let's talk: interview.

Directions: Ask two students each question. Write their answers in the chart. Share some of their answers with the class.

Question	Student A	Student B
1. What \ you \ like?		
2. What \ babies \ around the world \ like?		
3. What \ you \ want?		
4. What \ children around the world \ want?		
5. What \ you \ love?		
6. What \ teenagers around the world \ love?		
7. What \ you \ dislike or hate?		
8. What \ people around the world \ dislike or hate?		
9. What \ you \ need?		
10. What \ elderly people around the world \ need?		

4-7 SEE, LOOK AT, WATCH, HEAR, AND LISTEN TO

SEE, LOOK AT, and *WATCH* (a) I **see** many things in this room.	In (a): **see** = a nonaction verb. Seeing happens because my eyes are open. Seeing is a physical reaction, not a planned action.
(b) I'**m looking** at the clock. I want to know the time.	In (b): **look at** = an action verb. Looking is a planned or purposeful action. Looking happens for a reason.
(c) Bob **is watching** TV.	In (c): **watch** = an action verb. I *watch* something for a long time, but I *look at* something for a short time.
HEAR and *LISTEN TO* (d) I'm in my apartment. I'm trying to study. I **hear** music from the next apartment. The music is loud.	In (d): **hear** = a nonaction verb. Hearing is an unplanned act. It expresses a physical reaction.
(e) I'm in my apartment. I'm studying. I have a tape recorder. I'**m listening to** music. I like to listen to music when I study.	In (e): **listen (to)** = an action verb. Listening happens for a purpose.

□ EXERCISE 29. Let's talk: class activity.

Directions: Your teacher will ask you questions. Your book is closed.

Example:
TEACHER: Look at the floor. What do you see?
SPEAKER: I see shoes/dirt/etc.

1. What do you see in this room? Now look at something. What are you looking at?
2. Turn to p. 103 of this book. What do you see? Now look at one thing on that page. What are you looking at?
3. Look at the chalkboard. What do you see?
4. What programs do you like to watch on TV?
5. What sports do you like to watch?
6. What animals do you like to watch when you go to the zoo?
7. What do you hear at night in the place where you live?
8. What do you listen to when you go to a concert?
9. What do you listen to when you are at home?

☐ **EXERCISE 30. Verb review.**

    Directions: Complete the sentences with the words in parentheses. Use the simple present or the present progressive.

1. I *(sit)* _____*am sitting*_____ in class right now. I *(sit, always)*

    _____*always sit*_____ in the same seat every day.

2. Ali *(speak)* _____ Arabic, but right now he *(speak)*

    _____ English.

3. Right now we *(do)* _____ an exercise in class. We *(do)*

    _____ exercises in class every day.

4. I'm in class now. I *(look)* _____ at my classmates. Kim

    (write) _____ in his book. Francisco *(look)* _____

    _____ out the window. Yoko *(bite)* _____

    _____ her pencil. Abdullah *(smile)* _____.

    Maria *(sleep)* _____. Jung-Po *(chew)* _____

    _____ gum.

5. The person on the bench in the picture on p. 116 is Barbara. She's an accountant.

    She *(work)* _____ for the government. She *(have)* _____ an

    hour for lunch every day. She *(eat, often)* _____ lunch in

    the park. She *(bring, usually)* _____ a sandwich and

    some fruit with her to the park. She *(sit, usually)* _____

    on a bench, but sometimes she *(sit)* _____ on the grass. While she's at the

    park, she *(watch)* _____ people and animals. She *(watch)*

    _____ joggers and squirrels. She *(relax)* _____

    when she eats at the park.

6. Right now I *(look)* _____ at a picture of Barbara. She *(be, not)*

_____ at home in the picture. She *(be)* _____ at the park.

She *(sit)* _____ on a bench. She *(eat)* _____

_____ her lunch. A jogger *(run)* _____

on a path through the park. A squirrel *(sit)* _____ on the

ground in front of Barbara. The squirrel *(eat)* _____ a nut.

Barbara *(watch)* _____ the squirrel. She *(watch, always)*

_____ squirrels when she eats lunch in the park.

Some ducks *(swim)* _____ in the pond in the picture,

and some birds *(fly)* _____ in the sky. A police officer

(ride) _____ a horse. He *(ride)* _____ a

horse through the park every day. Near Barbara, a family *(have)* _____

_____ a picnic. They *(go)* _____ on a picnic every

week.

4-8 THINK ABOUT AND THINK THAT

	In (a): Ideas about my family are in my mind every day. In (b) My mind is busy now. Ideas about grammar are in my mind right now.
THINK + *ABOUT* + A NOUN (a) I *think* *about* *my family* every day. (b) I *am thinking* *about* *grammar* right now.	
THINK + *THAT* + A STATEMENT (c) I *think* *that* *Sue is lazy.* (d) Sue *thinks* *that* *I am lazy.* (e) I *think* *that* *the weather is nice.*	In (c): In my opinion, Sue is lazy. I believe that Sue is lazy. People use *think that* when they want to say (to state) their beliefs. The present progressive is often used with *think about*. The present progressive is almost never used with *think that*. INCORRECT: *I am thinking that Sue is lazy.*
(f) I *think that* Mike is a nice person. (g) I *think* Mike is a nice person.	(f) and (g) have the same meaning. People often omit *that* after *think*, especially in speaking.

□ EXERCISE 31. Sentence practice.

Directions: Use *I think (that)* to give your opinion. Share a few of your opinions with the class.

1. English grammar is easy / hard / fun / interesting. _____ *I think (that)* _____

   _____ *English grammar is* _____

2. People in this city are friendly / unfriendly / kind / cold.

   _____

3. The food at *(name of a place)* is delicious / terrible / good / excellent / awful.

   _____

4. Baseball / football / soccer / golf is interesting / boring / confusing / etc.

   _____

☐ EXERCISE 32. Sentence practice.
    Directions: Make sentences.

    PART I. Complete the sentences with your own words.

    1. I think that the weather today is _____

    2. I think my classmates are _____

    3. Right now I'm thinking about _____

    4. In my opinion, English grammar is _____

    5. In my opinion, soccer is _____

    6. I think that my parents are _____

    7. I think this school _____

    8. I think about _____

    9. I think that _____

    10. In my opinion, _____

    PART II. Share a few of your completions with the class.

☐ EXERCISE 33. Let's talk: small groups.
    Directions: Work in small groups. Take turns stating an opinion about each of the
    following topics.

    Example: books
    Response: I think that *War and Peace* is an excellent novel. OR
            In my opinion, *War and Peace* is an excellent novel.

    1. this city
    2. your English classes
    3. music
    4. movies
    5. cars
    6. the food in this country
    7. the weather in this area
    8. a current local, national, or international news story

□ EXERCISE 34. Chapter review.

Directions: Choose the correct completions.

1. Anita and Pablo _____ TV right now.
   A. watch   B. watching   Ⓒ are watching

2. "_____ you writing a letter to your parents?"
   "No. I'm studying."
   A. Do   B. Are   C. Don't

3. I _____ like to write letters.
   A. no   B. am not   C. don't

4. "Jack has six telephones in his apartment."
   "I _____ you. No one needs six telephones in one apartment."
   A. am believe   B. am not believing C. don't believe

5. When I want to know the time, I _____ a clock.
   A. see   B. look at   C. watch

6. "Do you know Fatima?"
   "Yes, I do. I _____ she is a very nice person."
   A. am thinking   B. thinking   C. think

7. Where _____ John? Upstairs or downstairs?
   A. does   B. is   C. lives

8. Oh no. Ron _____. He is allergic to cats.
   A. is sneezing   B. doesn't sneeze   C. sneezes

9. The teacher often _____ on time.
   A. doesn't start B. isn't starting   C. don't start

10. "You look sad."
    "Yes, I _____ about my family back in my country. I miss them."
    A. think   B. am thinking   C. thinking

□ EXERCISE 35. Chapter review: error analysis.

Directions: Correct the errors.

1. It's rainning today. I no like the rain.

2. I like New York City. I am thinking that it is a wonderful city.

3. Does Abdul be sleeping right now?

4. Why you are going downtown today?

5. I'm listening you.

6. Are you hearing a noise outside the window?

7. Kunio at a restaurant right now. He usually eat at home, but today he eatting dinner at a restaurant.

8. I am liking flowers. They are smelling good.

9. Alex is siting at his desk. He writting a letter.

10. Where do they are sitting today?

CHAPTER 5
Talking About the Present

☐ **EXERCISE 1. Preview: listening.**

👀 *Directions:* Write the answers to the questions.

Example:

You will hear: What time is it?

You will write: It's _____ *10:10 A.M. / around ten o'clock / etc.* _____.

1. It's _____.

2. It's _____.

3. It's _____.

4. It's _____.

5. It's _____.

5-1 USING *IT* TO TALK ABOUT TIME

QUESTION		ANSWER	
(a) What day is it?	→	*It's* Monday.	In English, people use *it* to express (to talk about) time.
(b) What month is it?	→	*It's* September.	
(c) What year is it?	→	*It's* 2_____.	
(d) What's the date today?	→	*It's* September 15th.	
	→	*It's* the 15th of September.	
(e) What time is it?	→	*It's* 9:00.★	
	→	*It's* nine.	
	→	*It's* nine o'clock.	
	→	*It's* nine (o'clock) A.M.	

★American English uses a colon (two dots) between the hour and the minutes: 9:00 A.M. British English uses one dot: 9.00 A.M.

☐ **EXERCISE 2. Question practice.**

Directions: Make questions. Begin each question with **What**.

1. A: _____*What day is it?*_____

    B: It's Tuesday.

2. A: _____

    B: It's March 14th.

3. A: _____

    B: Ten-thirty.

4. A: _____

    B: March.

5. A: _____

    B: It's six-fifteen.

6. A: _____

    B: Wednesday.

7. A: _____

    B: The 1st of April, 2 _____.

8. A: _____

    B: It's two thousand and _____.

9. A: _____

    B: It's seven A.M.

Sun	Mon	Tues	Wed	Thurs	Fri	Sat
				1	2	3
4	5	6	7	8	9	10
11	12	13	14	15	16	17
18	19	20	21	22	23	24
25	26	27	28	29	30	31

a calendar page

5-2 PREPOSITIONS OF TIME

at	(a) We have class **at** one o'clock. (b) I have an appointment with the doctor **at** 3:00. (c) We sleep **at** night.	**at** + a specific time on the clock. **at** + *night*
in	(d) My birthday is **in** October. (e) I was born **in** 1989. (f) We have class **in** the morning. (g) Bob has class **in** the afternoon. (h) I study **in** the evening.	**in** + a specific month **in** + a specific year **in** + *the morning* **in** + *the afternoon* **in** + *the evening*
on	(i) I have class **on** Monday. (j) I was born **on** October 31, 1991.	**on** + a specific day of the week **on** + a specific date
from ... to	(k) We have class **from** 1:00 **to** 2:00.	**from** (a specific time) **to** (a specific time)

☐ EXERCISE 3. Sentence practice.

Directions: Complete the sentences with prepositions of time.

1. We have class _____*at*_____ ten o'clock.

2. We have class _____ ten _____ eleven.

3. I have class _____ the morning, and I work _____ the afternoon.

4. I study _____ the evening.

5. I sleep _____ night.

6. I was born _____ May.

7. I was born _____ 1988.

8. I was born _____ May 21.

9. I was born _____ May 21, 1988.

10. The post office isn't open _____ Sundays.

11. The post office is open _____ 8:00 A.M. _____ 5:00 P.M. Monday through Saturday.

12. The post office closes _____ 5:00 P.M.

□ EXERCISE 4. Listening and sentence practice.
  Directions: Identify the people in the pictures.

👂 *PART I.* Listen to each description. Write the name of the person who is described.

Example:
You will hear: I was born on June 2, 1986. I go to class in the morning.
          My name is _____.
You will write: ___*Lisa*___

June 2, 1986 7:00 A.M.	June 24, 1980 1:00 P.M.	July 7, 1989 7:00 P.M.	July 24, 1990 11:00 A.M.
Lisa	Ann	Tom	Ron

1. _____

2. _____

3. _____

4. _____

PART II. Use the information in the pictures to complete the sentences.

1. I was born _____ July. I was born _____ July 7. My name is

   _____.

2. I was born _____ 1980. I was born _____ June 24, 1980. My

   name is _____.

3. I go to class _____ the morning. I go to class _____ 7:00. My

   name is _____.

4. Hi, my name is _____. I was born _____ July. I was born

   _____ July 24. I go to class _____ the morning.

5-3 USING *IT* TO TALK ABOUT THE WEATHER

(a) *It's* sunny today. (b) *It's* hot and humid today. (c) *It's* a nice day today.	In English, people usually use *it* when they talk about the weather.
(d) *What's the weather like* in Istanbul in January? (e) *How's the weather* in Moscow in the summer?	People commonly ask about the weather by saying *What's the weather like?* OR *How's the weather?*

☐ EXERCISE 5. Let's talk: pairwork.

Directions: How's the weather today? Circle *yes* or *no*. Share your answers with a partner. Do your answers agree? Report to the class.

1. hot	yes	no	8. sunny	yes	no
2. warm	yes	no	9. nice	yes	no
3. cool	yes	no	10. clear	yes	no
4. chilly	yes	no	11. partly cloudy	yes	no
5. cold	yes	no	12. humid★	yes	no
6. freezing	yes	no	13. windy	yes	no
7. below freezing	yes	no	14. stormy	yes	no

☐ EXERCISE 6. Let's talk: small groups.

Directions: Change the Fahrenheit (F) temperatures to Celsius (C) by choosing temperatures from the list. Then describe the temperature in words.

38° C	24° C	✓10° C	0° C	− 18° C

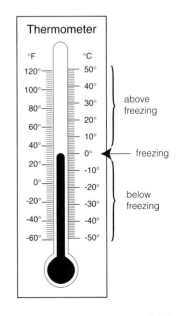

FAHRENHEIT CELSIUS   DESCRIPTION

1. 50° F   _10°C_   _cool, chilly_

2. 32° F   _____   _____

3. 100° F _____   _____

4. 75° F   _____   _____

5. 0° F   _____   _____

★*humid* = hot and wet

☐ EXERCISE 7. Let's talk: small groups.

> *Directions:* Work in small groups. Read the chart and follow the instructions.

"Approximate" means "close but not exact." Here is a fast way to get an **approximate** number when you convert from one temperature system to another.*

• To change **Celsius to Fahrenheit**: DOUBLE THE CELSIUS NUMBER AND ADD 30.

> *Examples:*   12°C × 2 = 24 + 30 =   54°F. (Exact numbers: 12°C = 53.6°F.)
>   20°C × 2 = 40 + 30 =   70°F. (Exact numbers: 20°C = 68°F.)
>   35°C × 2 = 70 + 30 = 100°F. (Exact numbers: 35°C = 95°F.)

• To change **Fahrenheit to Celsius**: SUBTRACT 30 FROM THE FAHRENHEIT NUMBER AND THEN DIVIDE BY 2.

> *Examples:*   60°F − 30 = 30 ÷ 2 = 15°C. (Exact numbers: 60°F = 15.6°C.)
>   80°F − 30 = 50 ÷ 2 = 25°C. (Exact numbers: 80°F = 26.7°C.)
>   90°F − 30 = 60 ÷ 2 = 30°C. (Exact numbers: 90°F = 32.2°C.)

*To get exact numbers, use these formulas: C = 5/9 (°F − 32) OR F = 9/5 (°C) + 32.

Change the following from Celsius to Fahrenheit and Fahrenheit to Celsius. Calculate the **approximate** numbers.

1.   22°C →   *22°C = approximately 74°F (22°C x 2 = 44 + 30 = 74°F)*

2.   2°C → _____

3.   30°C → _____

4.   10°C → _____

5.   16°C → _____

6.   45°F → _____

7.   70°F → _____

8.   58°F → _____

9. 100°F → _____

10.   20°F → _____

□ EXERCISE 8. Interview and paragraph practice.

Directions: Find out information about your classmates' hometowns. Use the information to write a report. Ask questions about *the name of the hometown, its location, its population, its weather and average temperature in a particular month (of your choosing).*

Example:

SPEAKER A: What's your hometown?

SPEAKER B: Athens.

SPEAKER A: Where is it located?

SPEAKER B: In southeastern Greece near the Aegean Sea.

SPEAKER A: What's the population of Athens?

SPEAKER B: Almost four million.

SPEAKER A: What's the weather like in Athens in May?

SPEAKER B: It's mild. Sometimes it's a little rainy.

SPEAKER A: What's the average temperature in May?

SPEAKER B: The average temperature is around 21° Celsius.

Chart for recording information about three of your classmates' hometowns.

Name	*Spyros*			
Hometown	*Athens*			
Location	*SE Greece*			
Population	*almost 4 million*			
Weather	*mild in May, around 21°C, in the mid-seventies Fahrenheit*			

5-4 THERE + BE

THERE + BE + SUBJECT + PLACE
(a) **There** *is* *a bird* in the tree.
(b) **There** *are* *four birds* in the tree.
	There + be is used to say that something exists in a particular place.
	Notice: The subject follows **be:**
	   there + is + singular noun
	   there + are + plural noun

(c) **There's** a bird in the tree.
(d) **There're** four birds in the tree.
	CONTRACTIONS:
	   there + is = there's
	   there + are = there're

☐ EXERCISE 9. Sentence practice.

Directions: Complete the sentences with *is* or *are*. Then circle *yes* or *no*. Compare your answers with your classmates' answers.

1. There _____ *is* _____ a butterfly in this picture.   (yes)   no

2. There _____ *are* _____ two trees in this picture.   yes   (no)

3. There _____ a bird in this picture.   yes   no

4. There _____ seven flowers in this picture.   yes   no

5. There _____ a grammar book on my desk.   yes   no

6. There _____ many grammar books in this room.   yes   no

7. There _____ comfortable chairs in this classroom.   yes   no

8. There _____ a nice view from the classroom window.   yes   no

9. There _____ interesting places to visit in this area.   yes   no

10. There _____ a good place to eat near school.   yes   no

11. There _____ fun activities to do on weekends in this area.   yes   no

12. There _____ difficult words in this exercise.   yes   no

☐ EXERCISE 10. Let's talk: pairwork.

Directions: Work with a partner. Complete the sentences with the words in the list or your own words. When you speak, look at your partner.

a book	*a map*	*a notebook*
some books	*some papers*	*some notebooks*
tall buildings	*a park*	*some restaurants*
a bulletin board	*a pen*	*a sink*
a calendar	*a pencil*	*many stores*
some chairs	*a pencil sharpener*	*several students*
a chalkboard	*many people*	*a teacher*
a clock	*a picture*	*a whiteboard*
a coffee shop	*some pictures*	*a window*
some desks	*a post office*	*some windows*
some light switches		

1. PARTNER A: There is . . . on this desk.
   PARTNER B: There are . . . on that desk.

2. PARTNER A: There are . . . on that wall.
   PARTNER B: There is . . . on this wall.

3. PARTNER A: There are . . . in this room.
   PARTNER B: There is also . . . in this room.

4. PARTNER A: There is . . . near our school.
   PARTNER B: There are also . . . near our school.

☐ EXERCISE 11. Let's talk: small groups.

Directions: Work in small groups. After everybody puts two or three objects (e.g., a coin, some keys, a pen, a dictionary) on a table in the classroom, describe the items on the table. Use **There is . . . .** and **There are . . . .**

Examples:
SPEAKER A: There are three dictionaries on the table.
SPEAKER B: There are some keys on the table.
SPEAKER C: There is a pencil sharpener on the table.

☐ EXERCISE 12. Listening.

Directions: Listen to each sentence. Circle the word you hear. Note: You will hear contractions for **There is** and **There are**.

Example: _____ several windows in this room.   There's   (There're)

1. There's	There're	5. There's	There're
2. There's	There're	6. There's	There're
3. There's	There're	7. There's	There're
4. There's	There're	8. There's	There're

☐ EXERCISE 13. Let's talk: small groups.

Directions: Work in small groups. Choose a leader. Take turns making sentences. Begin your sentence with **There**.

Example:
 LEADER: . . . in this building.
SPEAKER A: There are five floors in this building.
SPEAKER B: There are many classrooms in this building.
SPEAKER C: There are stairs in this building.
 LEADER: There is an elevator in this building.
Etc.

1. . . . in my home.
2. . . . in this city.
3. . . . in my country.
4. . . . in the world.
5. . . . in the universe.

5-5 *THERE + BE:* YES/NO QUESTIONS

			QUESTION			SHORT ANSWER
BE	+	*THERE*	+	SUBJECT		
(a) **Is**		**there**		**any juice**	in the refrigerator? →	Yes, **there is**.
					→	No, **there isn't**.
(b) **Are**		**there**		**any eggs**	in the refrigerator? →	Yes, **there are**.
					→	No, **there aren't**.

☐ **EXERCISE 14. Let's talk: pairwork.**

Directions: Work with a partner. Ask questions about the contents of the refrigerator in the picture. Use the nouns in the list in your questions. Use ***Is there . . . ?*** or ***Are there . . . ?***

Example:

PARTNER A: Is there any cheese in the refrigerator?
PARTNER B: Yes, there is.
PARTNER A: Your turn now.
PARTNER B: Are there any onions in the refrigerator?
PARTNER A: No, there aren't.
PARTNER B: Your turn now.

Partner A
1. cheese
2. eggs
3. bread
4. apples
5. butter
6. potatoes
7. vegetables

Partner B
1. onions
2. strawberries
3. oranges
4. orange juice
5. fruit
6. flour
7. pickles

☐ **EXERCISE 15. Let's talk: small groups.**

Directions: Work in small groups. Take turns asking and answering questions using ***there + be***. Ask questions about this city. Use ***Is there . . . ?*** or ***Are there . . . ?*** If the answer is "I don't know," ask someone else.

Example: a zoo

SPEAKER A: Is there a zoo in *(name of this city)?*
SPEAKER B: Yes, there is. / No, there isn't.
SPEAKER B: *(to Speaker C)* Is there an airport near *(name of this city)?*
SPEAKER C: I don't know.
SPEAKER B: *(to Speaker D)* Is there an airport near *(name of this city)?*
SPEAKER D: Yes, there is. / No, there isn't.
Etc.

1. a zoo
2. an airport
3. any lakes
4. any good restaurants
5. a good Chinese restaurant
6. an art museum
7. an aquarium
8. any interesting bookstores
9. a subway system
10. any public swimming pools
11. a good public transportation system
12. any movie theaters

☐ EXERCISE 16. Let's talk: class activity.

Directions: Solve the puzzle. Teacher's Note: Use the grid on p. 509 of the *Answer Key* to answer your students' questions.

The Johnson family needs to decide where to stay for their summer vacation. They want a hotel that has everything in the list below. Your teacher has information about several hotels. Ask her/him questions using the list. Then write *yes* or *no* in the correct column of the chart. Which hotel has everything that the Johnsons want?

Example:

SPEAKER A: Is there a swimming pool at Hotel 1?
  TEACHER: Yes, there is.
SPEAKER B: Are there tennis courts at Hotel 3?
  TEACHER: Yes, there are.
SPEAKER C: Are there ocean-view rooms at Hotel 5?
  TEACHER: Yes, there are.

LIST	
a beach	a swimming pool
horses to ride	tennis courts
ocean-view rooms	

CHART					
	a swimming pool	a beach	tennis courts	horses	ocean-view rooms
HOTEL 1	yes				
HOTEL 2		yes			
HOTEL 3			yes		
HOTEL 4				yes	
HOTEL 5					yes

5-6 THERE + BE: ASKING QUESTIONS WITH HOW MANY

QUESTION	SHORT ANSWER
HOW MANY + SUBJECT + *ARE* + *THERE* + PLACE (a) ***How many*** ***chapters*** ***are*** ***there*** in this book? → Sixteen. (There are 16 chapters in this book.) (b) ***How many*** ***provinces*** ***are*** ***there*** in Canada? → Ten. (There are ten provinces in Canada.)	
(c) How many ***words*** do you see? INCORRECT: *How many word do you see?*	Notice: The noun that follows ***how many*** is plural.

☐ EXERCISE 17. Let's talk: class activity.
Directions: Ask and answer questions about this room. Use ***How many*** and the given words.

Example: desks
SPEAKER A: How many desks are there in this room?
SPEAKER B: Thirty-two. OR There are thirty-two desks in this room.
SPEAKER A: That's right. OR No, I count thirty-three desks.

1. windows
2. desks
3. students
4. teachers
5. women
6. men
7. grammar books
8. dictionaries

☐ EXERCISE 18. Let's talk: pairwork.
Directions: Work with a partner. Ask questions with ***How many***.

Example: days in a week
PARTNER A: How many days are there in a week?
PARTNER B: Seven. OR There are seven days in a week.
PARTNER A: Right. There are seven days in a week. Your turn now.

Partner A
1. chapters in this book
2. doors in this room
3. floors in this building
4. states in the United States (50)
5. countries in North America (3)

Partner B
1. pages in this book
2. people in this room
3. letters in the English alphabet (26)
4. provinces in Canada (10)
5. continents in the world (7)

5-7 PREPOSITIONS OF PLACE

(a) My book is **on** my desk.	In (a): *on* = a preposition *my desk* = object of the preposition *on my desk* = a prepositional phrase

(b) Tom lives **in** *the United States.*
He lives **in** *New York City.*
(c) He lives **on** *Hill Street.*
(d) He lives **at** *4472 Hill Street.*
	A person lives: **in** a country and **in** a city
	      on a street, avenue, road, etc.
	      at a street address
	(See Chart 12-9, p. 374, for more information
	about using **in** and **at**.)

Note: Prepositions of place are also called "prepositions of location."

□ **EXERCISE 19. Sentence practice.**
  Directions: Complete the sentences with **in, on,** or **at**.

Write about Pablo.

1. Pablo lives _____ Canada.

2. He lives _____ Toronto.

3. He lives _____ Lake Street.

4. He lives _____ 5541 Lake Street

  _____ Toronto, Canada.

Write about Dr. Lee.

5. Dr. Lee lives on _____.

6. He lives in _____.

7. He lives at _____.

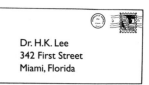

Write about yourself.

8. I live _____.
        (name of country)

9. I live _____.
        (name of city)

10. I live _____.
        (name of street)

11. I live _____.
        (street address)

5-8 SOME PREPOSITIONS OF PLACE: A LIST

above	*beside*	*in back of*	*in the middle of*	*on*
around	*between*	*in the back of*	*inside*	*on top of*
at	*far (away) from*	*in front of*	*near*	*outside*
behind	*in*	*in the front of*	*next to*	*under*
below				

(a) The book is **beside** the cup.

(b) The book is **next to** the cup.

(c) The book is **near** the cup.

(d) The book is **between** two cups.

(e) The book is **far away from** the cup.

(f) The cup is **on** the book.

(g) The cup is **on top of** the book.

(h) The cup is **under** the book.

(i) The cup is **above** the book.

(j) The hand is **around** the cup.

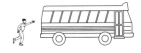

(k) The man is **in back of** the bus.

(l) The man is **behind** the bus.

(m) The man is **in the back of** the bus.

(n) The man is **in front of** the bus.
In (k), (l), and (n): the man is **outside** the bus.

(o) The man is **in the front of** the bus.

(p) The man is **in the middle of** the bus.
In (m), (o), and (p): the man is **inside** the bus.

☐ EXERCISE 20. Sentence practice.

Directions: Describe the pictures by completing the sentences with prepositional expressions of place. There may be more than one possible completion.

1. The apple is ___on, on top of___ the plate.

2. The apple is _____ the plate.

3. The apple is _____ the plate.

4. The apple is _____ the glass.

5. The apple isn't near the glass. It is _____ _____ the glass.

6. The apple is _____ the glass.

7. The apple is _____ two glasses.

8. The hand is _____ the glass.

9. The dog isn't inside the car. The dog is _____ the car.

10. The dog is in _____ of the car.

11. The dog is in _____ of the car.

12. The dog is in _____ of the car.

13. The dog is in _____ of the car.

☐ **EXERCISE 21. Let's talk: pairwork.**

Directions: Work with a partner. Choose a small object (a pen, pencil, coin, etc.). Give and follow directions. You can look at your book before you speak. When you speak, look at your partner.

Partner A: Give your partner directions. Your book is open.
Partner B: Follow the directions. Your book is closed.

Example: (a small object such as a coin)
PARTNER A *(book open):* Put it on top of the desk.
PARTNER B *(book closed): (Partner B puts the coin on top of the desk.)*

1. Put it on your head.
2. Put it above your head.
3. Put it between your fingers.
4. Put it near me.
5. Put it far away from me.
6. Put it under your book.
7. Put it below your knee.
8. Put it in the middle of your grammar book.

Switch roles.
Partner A: Close your book.
Partner B: Open your book. Your turn to give directions.

9. Put it inside your grammar book.
10. Put it next to your grammar book.
11. Put it on top of your grammar book.
12. Put it in front of me.
13. Put it behind me.
14. Put it in back of your back.
15. Put it in the back of your grammar book.
16. Put your hand around it.

☐ **EXERCISE 22. Let's talk: pairwork.**

Directions: Work with a partner. Ask and answer questions about the picture. Practice using *Is there / Are there*, *Where*, and *How many*. Use the vocabulary in the list to help you.

bikes	*cars*	*flowers*	*a picnic bench*
a bird	*chickens*	*a guitar*	*a picnic table*
a boat	*clouds*	*hills*	*rabbits*
boots	*dogs*	*a knife*	*a river*
a bridge	*a fish*	*motorcycles*	*a train*
butterflies	*a fishing pole*	*people*	*trees*

Example:

PARTNER A: **Are there** any dogs in the picture?
PARTNER B: No, there aren't any dogs in the picture.
PARTNER A: Your turn to ask.

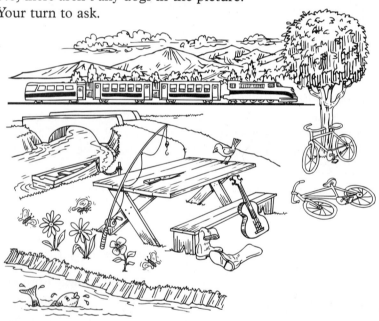

☐ **EXERCISE 23. Listening.**

Directions: Listen to the sentences about the picture in Exercise 22. Circle the correct answers.

Example: The bike is in the water.   yes   (no)

1. yes no	6. yes no	11. yes no
2. yes no	7. yes no	12. yes no
3. yes no	8. yes no	13. yes no
4. yes no	9. yes no	14. yes no
5. yes no	10. yes no	15. yes no

☐ EXERCISE 24. Review: Chapters 4 and 5.

Directions: Talk about the picture below. Use the vocabulary in the list to help you answer the questions.

burn	*a bowl*	*meat*
eat dinner	*a bowl of salad*	*a piece of meat*
have a steak for dinner	*a candle*	*a plate*
hold a knife and a fork	*a cup*	*a restaurant*
	a cup of coffee	*a saucer*
	a fork	*a spoon*
	a glass	*a steak*
	a glass of water	*a table*
	a knife	*a waiter*
	a vase of flowers	

PART I. Work in pairs or as a class. Answer the questions. (Alternate questions if working in pairs.)

1. What is Mary doing?
2. What do you see on the table?
3. What is Mary holding in her right hand? in her left hand?
4. What is in the bowl?
5. What is on the plate?
6. What is in the cup?
7. What is burning?
8. Is Mary eating breakfast?
9. Is Mary at home? Where is she?
10. What is she cutting?

PART II. Complete the sentences.

11. Mary is sitting _____ a table.

12. There is a candle _____ the table.

13. There is coffee _____ the cup.

14. Mary _____ holding a knife _____ her right hand.

15. She's _____ a restaurant.

16. She _____ at home.

17. She _____ eating breakfast.

☐ **EXERCISE 25. Review: Chapters 4 and 5.**

Directions: Talk about the picture below. Use the vocabulary in the list to help you answer the questions.

read a book	the circulation desk
study at the library	a librarian
take notes	a shelf (singular)
	shelves (plural)★

PART I. Work in pairs or as a class. Answer the questions. (Alternate questions if working in pairs.)

1. What is John doing?
2. What do you see in the picture?
3. Is John at home? Where is he?
4. Is John reading a newspaper?
5. Where is the librarian standing?
6. Is John right-handed or left-handed?

PART II. Complete the sentences.

7. John is studying _____ the library.

8. He is sitting _____ a table.

9. He is sitting _____ a chair.

10. His legs are _____ the table.

11. There are books _____ the shelves.

12. John is writing _____ a piece of paper.

13. He's taking notes _____ a piece of paper.

14. He _____ reading a newspaper.

15. The librarian _____

    standing _____

    the circulation desk.

16. Another student is sitting

    _____ John.

_____

★See Chart 6-5, p. 173, for information about nouns with irregular plural forms.

☐ EXERCISE 26. Review: Chapters 4 and 5.

Directions: Talk about the picture. Use the vocabulary in the list to help you **answer** the questions.

the date	*a bank*	*first name / given name*
sign a check	*cash*	*middle initial*
sign her name	*a check*	*last name / family name / surname*
write a check★		*name and address*

PART I. Work in pairs or as a class. Answer the questions. (Alternate questions if working in pairs.)

1. What is Mary doing?
2. What is Mary's address?
3. What is Mary's full name?
4. What is Mary's middle initial?
5. What is Mary's last name?
6. How much money does Mary want?

7. What is in the upper-left corner of the check?
8. What is in the lower-left corner of the check?
9. What is the name of the bank?

```
MARY S. JONES
3471 TREE ST.
CHICAGO, IL 60565                              May 3, 2005

PAY TO THE    Cash
ORDER OF                                    $  50.00

Fifty and 00/100                                      DOLLARS

FIRST NATIONAL BANK
605 MICHIGAN AVE.
CHICAGO, IL 60503                           Mary S. Jones

I:021 200911 438 200
```

PART II. Complete the sentences.

10. Mary is writing a _____ .

11. She is signing _____ name.

12. The name _____ the bank is First National Bank.

13. Mary lives _____ 3471 Tree Street.

14. Mary lives _____ Chicago, Illinois.

15. Mary's name and address are _____ the upper-left corner _____ the check.

★*Check* (American English) is spelled *cheque* in British and Canadian English. The pronunciation of *check* and *cheque* is the same.

☐ **EXERCISE 27. Review: Chapters 4 and 5.**

Directions: Talk about the picture below. Use the vocabulary in the list to help you answer the questions.

cash a check	a bank teller	a man (singular)
stand in line	a counter	men (plural)★
	a line	people (plural)★
		a woman (singular)
		women (plural)★

PART I. Work in pairs or as a class. Answer the questions. (Alternate questions if working in pairs.)

1. What is Mary doing?
2. Is Mary at a store? Where is she?
3. What do you see in the picture?
4. Who is standing behind Mary, a man or a woman?
5. Who is standing at the end of the line, a man or a woman?

6. How many men are there in the picture?
7. How many women are there in the picture?
8. How many people are there in the picture?
9. How many people are standing in line?

PART II. Complete the sentences.

10. Mary is _____ a bank.

11. Four people _____ standing in line.

12. Mary is standing _____ the counter.

13. The bank teller is standing _____ the counter.

14. A woman _____ standing _____ Mary.

15. Mary _____ standing _____

 the end _____ the line.

16. A man _____ standing _____

 the end _____ the line.

17. A businessman _____

 standing_____ the woman

 in the dress and the young man with the beard.

_____

*See Chart 6-5, p. 173, for information about nouns with irregular plural forms.

5-9 *NEED* AND *WANT* + A NOUN OR AN INFINITIVE

		VERB	+	NOUN		*Need* is stronger than *want*. *Need* gives the idea that something is very important.
(a)	We	*need*		*food*.		
(b)	I	*want*		*a sandwich*.		*Need* and *want* are followed by a noun or by an infinitive.
		VERB	+	INFINITIVE		An infinitive = *to* + *the simple form of a verb.* ★
(c)	We	*need*		*to eat*.		
(d)	I	*want*		*to eat* a sandwich.		

★The simple form of a verb = a verb without *-s, -ed*, or *-ing*. Examples of the simple form of a verb: *come, help, answer, write.*
Examples of infinitives: *to come, to help, to answer, to write.*

☐ EXERCISE 28. Sentence practice.
> *Directions:* Add *to* where necessary.

1. I want some water. *(no change)*

2. I want _∧ drink some water.
           to

3. Linda wants go to the bookstore.

4. Linda wants a new dictionary.

5. I need make a telephone call.

6. I need a telephone.

7. Do you want go to the movie with us?

8. Do you need a new notebook?

☐ EXERCISE 29. Let's talk: class activity.
> *Directions:* Your teacher will ask you questions using *need* and *want*. Think about your day tomorrow. Close your book for this activity.

> *Example:*
> TEACHER: What do you need to do tomorrow morning?
> STUDENT A: I need to go to school at 8:00.
> TEACHER: *(to Student B)* What do you need to do?
> STUDENT B: I need to eat breakfast.
> TEACHER: *(to Student C)* What does *(Student B)* need to do?
> STUDENT C: He/She needs to eat breakfast.

What do you . . .

1. need to do tomorrow morning?

2. want to do tomorrow morning?

3. need to do in the afternoon tomorrow?

4. want to do in the afternoon?

5. want to do in the evening?

6. need to do tomorrow evening?

□ EXERCISE 30. Sentence practice.
Directions: Use the words in the list or your own words to complete the sentences. Use an infinitive *(to* + verb) in each sentence. Some words can be used more than once.

buy	go	pay	walk
call	listen to	play	wash
cash	marry	take	watch
do			

1. Anna is sleepy. She wants _____to go_____ to bed.

2. I want _____ downtown today because I need _____

   a new coat.

3. Mike wants _____ TV. There's a good program on Channel 5.

4. Do you want _____ soccer with us at the park this afternoon?

5. I need _____ Jennifer on the phone.

6. I want _____ to the bank because I need _____ a check.

7. James doesn't want _____ his homework tonight.

8. My clothes are dirty. I need _____ them.

9. John loves Mary. He wants _____ her.

10. Helen needs _____ an English course.

11. Where do you want _____ for lunch?

12. Do you want _____ some music on the radio?

13. It's a nice day. I don't want _____
    the bus home today. I want _____
    home instead.

14. David's desk is full of overdue bills. He needs
    _____ his bills.

☐ EXERCISE 31. Listening.

Directions: Listen to the conversations and complete the sentences.

Example:
You will hear: Do you want to go downtown this afternoon?
You will write: _____*Do you want to go*_____ downtown this afternoon?
You will hear: Yes, I do. I need to buy a winter coat.
You will write: Yes, I do. _____*I need to buy*_____ a winter coat.

1. A: Where _____ for dinner tonight?
   B: Rossini's Restaurant.

2. A: What time _____ to the airport?
   B: Around five. My plane leaves at seven.

3. A: Jean _____ to the baseball game.
   B: Why not?
   A: Because _____ for a test.

4. A: I'm getting tired. _____ a break for a few
      minutes.
   B: Okay. Let's take a break. We can finish the work later.

5. A: _____ to class on Friday.
   B: Why not?
   A: It's a holiday.

6. A: Peter _____ to his
      apartment.
   B: Why?
   A: Because _____ his
      clothes before he goes to the party.

7. A: Where _____ for your vacation?

   B: _____ Niagara Falls, Quebec, and
   Montreal.

8. A: May I see your dictionary? _____ a word.
   B: Of course. Here it is.
   A: Thanks.

9. A: _____ with us to the park?

   B: Sure. Thanks. _____ some exercise.

5-10   WOULD LIKE

(a) I'm thirsty. I *want* a glass of water. (b) I'm thirsty. I *would like* a glass of water.	(a) and (b) have the same meaning, but *would like* is usually more polite than *want*. *I would like* is a nice way of saying *I want*.
(c) *I would like* *You would like* *She would like* *He would like* *We would like* *They would like* } a glass of water.	Notice in (c): There is no final *-s* on *would*. There is no final *-s* on *like*.
(d) CONTRACTIONS *I'd* = *I would* *you'd* = *you would* *she'd* = *she would* *he'd* = *he would* *we'd* = *we would* *they'd* = *they would*	*Would* is often contracted with pronouns in both speaking and writing. In speaking, *would* is usually contracted with nouns too. WRITTEN: Tom would like to come. SPOKEN: "Tom'd like to come."
WOULD LIKE + INFINITIVE (e) I *would like* *to eat* a sandwich.	Notice in (e): *would like* can be followed by an infinitive.
WOULD + SUBJECT + LIKE (f) *Would* you *like* some tea?	In a question, *would* comes before the subject.
(g) Yes, I *would*. (I would like some tea.)	*Would* is used alone in short answers to questions with *would like*. It is not contracted in short answers.

☐ EXERCISE 32. Sentence practice and listening activity.

Directions: Make sentences.

PART I. Change the sentences by using *would like*.

1. **Tony wants** a cup of coffee.

   → ___*Tony would like* OR *Tony'd like*___ a cup of coffee.

2. **He wants** some sugar in his coffee.

   → ___*He would like* OR *He'd like*___ some sugar in his coffee.

3. **Ahmed and Anita want** some coffee too.

   → _____ some coffee too.

4. **They want** some sugar in their coffee too.

   → _____ some sugar in their coffee too.

5. A: **Do you want** a cup of coffee?

   B: Yes, **I do.** Thank you.

   → A: _____ a cup of coffee?

   B: Yes, _____. Thank you.

6. **I want to thank** you for your kindness and hospitality.

   → _____ you for your kindness and hospitality.

7. **My friends want to thank** you too.

   → _____ you too.

8. A: **Does Robert want to ride** with us?

   B: Yes, **he does.**

   → A: _____ with us?

   B: Yes, _____.

🎧 **PART II.** Listen to the sentences for contractions with *would*. Practice repeating them.

□ EXERCISE 33. Let's talk: class activity.

Directions: Your teacher will ask you questions. Close your book for this activity.

1. Who's hungry right now? (. . .), are you hungry? What would you like?
2. Who's thirsty? (. . .), are you thirsty? What would you like?
3. Who's sleepy? What would you like to do?
4. What would you like to do this weekend?
5. What would you like to do after class today?
6. What would you like to have for dinner tonight?
7. What countries would you like to visit?
8. What cities would you like to visit in *(the United States, Canada, etc.)?*
9. What languages would you like to learn?
10. You listened to your classmates. What would they like to do? Do you remember what they said?
11. Pretend that you are a host at a party at your home and your classmates are your guests. Ask them what they would like to eat or drink.
12. Think of something fun to do tonight or this weekend. Using *would you like,* invite a classmate to join you.

5-11 *WOULD LIKE* vs. *LIKE*

(a) I ***would like to go*** to the zoo. (b) I ***like to go*** to the zoo.	In (a): *I would like to go to the zoo* means *I want to go to the zoo.* In (b): *I like to go to the zoo* means *I enjoy the zoo.* ***Would like*** indicates that I want to do something now or in the future. ***Like*** indicates that I always, usually, or often enjoy something.

□ EXERCISE 34. Listening.

Directions: Listen to the sentences and circle the verbs you hear. Some sentences have contractions.

Example: I _____ some tea.　　　　like　　　('d like)

1. like	'd like		6. likes	'd like
2. like	'd like		7. like	'd like
3. like	'd like		8. like	'd like
4. likes	'd like		9. like	'd like
5. like	'd like		10. like	'd like

☐ EXERCISE 35. Let's talk: class activity.

Directions: Discuss possible completions for the sentences. Use your own words.

1. I need to _____ every day.

2. I want to _____ today.

3. I like to _____ every day.

4. I would like to _____ today.

5. I don't like to _____ every day.

6. I don't want to _____ today.

7. Do you like to _____ ?

8. Would you like to _____ ?

9. I need to _____ and _____ today.

10. _____ would you like to _____ this evening?

☐ EXERCISE 36. Let's talk: pairwork.

Directions: Work in pairs. Ask and answer questions. Look at your partner when you speak.

Example:
PARTNER A: Do you like apples?
PARTNER B: Yes, I do. OR No, I don't.
PARTNER A: Would you like an apple right now?
PARTNER B: Yes, I would. OR Yes, thank you. OR No, but thank you for asking.
PARTNER A: Your turn now.

Partner A	Partner B
1. Do you like coffee ? Would you like a cup of coffee?	1. Do you like chocolate? Would you like some chocolate right now?
2. Do you like to go to movies? Would you like to go to a movie with me later today?	2. Do you like to go shopping? Would you like to go shopping with me later today?
3. What do you like to do on weekends? What would you like to do this weekend?	3. What do you like to do in your free time? What would you like to do in your free time tomorrow?
4. What do you need to do this evening? What would you like to do this evening?	4. Do you like to travel? What countries would you like to visit?

☐ **EXERCISE 37. Review: Chapters 4 and 5.**

Directions: Talk about the picture below. Use the vocabulary in the list to help you answer the questions.

cook	*a kitchen*	*bread*
cook dinner	*a list/a grocery list*	*butter*
make dinner	*a pepper shaker*	*coffee*
taste (food)	*a pot*	*an egg*
	a refrigerator	*pepper*
	a salt shaker	*salt*
	a stove	

PART I. Work in pairs or as a class. Answer the questions. (Alternate questions if working in pairs.)

1. What is John doing?
2. What do you see in the picture?
3. Where is John?
4. Is John tasting his dinner?
5. Is John a good cook?

6. Where is the refrigerator?
7. What is on the refrigerator?
8. Is the food on the stove hot or cold?
9. Is the food in the refrigerator hot or cold?

PART II. Complete the sentences.

10. John is making dinner. He's _____ the kitchen.

11. There is a pot _____ the stove.

12. The stove is _____ the refrigerator.

13. There is a grocery list _____ the refrigerator door.

14. John needs _____ to the grocery store.

15. A salt shaker and a pepper shaker are _____ the stove.

16. There is hot food _____ top _____ the stove.

17. There is cold food _____ the refrigerator.

☐ EXERCISE 38. Review: Chapters 4 and 5.

Directions: Talk about the picture below. Use the vocabulary in the list to help you answer the questions.

sing	*a cat*	*a living room*
sit on a sofa	*a dog*	*a rug*
sleep	*a fish*	*a singer*
swim	*a fishbowl*	*a sofa*
watch TV/television	*a floor*	*a TV set/a television set*
	a lamp	

PART I. Work in pairs or as a class. Answer the questions. (Alternate questions if working in pairs.)

1. What are John and Mary doing?
2. What do you see in the picture?
3. Are John and Mary in the kitchen? Where are they?
4. Where is the lamp?
5. Where is the rug?
6. Where is the dog?
7. Where is the cat?
8. Is the cat walking? What is the cat doing?
9. What is the dog doing?
10. What is on top of the TV set?
11. Is the fish watching TV?
12. What is on the TV screen? What are John and Mary watching?

PART II. Complete the sentences.

13. John and Mary _____ watching TV. They like _____ watch TV.

14. They _____ sitting _____ a sofa.

15. They _____ sleeping.

16. There is a rug _____ the floor.

17. A dog _____ sleeping _____ the rug.

18. A cat _____ sleeping _____

    the sofa.

□ EXERCISE 39. Review: Chapters 4 and 5.

Directions: Talk about the picture below. Use the vocabulary in the list to help you answer the questions.

draw a picture	an arrow	a piece of paper
smile	a calendar	a telephone book
talk on the phone	a heart	a wall
talk to (someone)	a phone/a telephone	
talk to each other	a picture	
	a picture of a mountain	

PART I. Work in pairs or as a class. Answer the questions. (Alternate questions if working in pairs.)

1. What are John and Mary doing?
2. What do you see in the picture?
3. Is John happy? Is Mary happy? Are John and Mary smiling?
4. Are they sad?
5. Who is standing? Who is sitting?
6. Is John in his bedroom? Where is John?

7. What is Mary drawing?
8. What is on Mary's table?
9. What is on the wall next to the refrigerator?
10. Where is the clock?
11. What time is it?
12. What is on the wall above the table?

PART II. Complete the sentences.

13. John and Mary _____ talking _____ the phone.

14. John _____ talking _____ Mary. Mary _____ talking _____ John.

    They _____ talking to _____ other.

15. John is _____ the kitchen. He's standing _____ the refrigerator.

16. There is a calendar _____ the wall next to the refrigerator.

17. Mary _____ sitting _____ a table. She's _____ a picture.

18. Mary likes to _____ to John on the phone.

19. There is a telephone book _____ the table.

20. There is picture _____ a mountain _____ the table.

☐ EXERCISE 40. Review: Chapters 4 and 5.

Directions: Talk about the picture below. Use the vocabulary in the list to help you answer the questions.

sleep	*a bed*
dream	*a dream*
dream about (someone/something)	*a head*
	a pillow

PART I. Work in pairs or as a class. Answer the questions. (Alternate questions if working in pairs.)

1. What is Mary doing?
2. What is John doing?
3. What are Mary and John doing?
4. What do you see in the picture?
5. Is Mary in her bedroom?
6. Is John in class? Where is he?
7. Is John standing or lying down?
8. Is Mary dreaming?
9. Are Mary and John dreaming about each other?
10. Are John and Mary in love?

PART II. Complete the sentences.

11. John and Mary _____ sleeping. They are _____ bed.

12. John _____ dreaming _____ Mary. Mary _____ dreaming

    _____ John. They _____ dreaming _____ each other.

13. Mary's head is _____ a pillow.

14. John and Mary _____ in the living room.

15. They _____ asleep. They _____ awake.

16. John and Mary love each other. They are _____ love.

17. They would like _____ get married someday.

☐ EXERCISE 41. Let's talk: pairwork.

> *Directions:* Work with a partner. Bring to class one or two pictures of your country (or any interesting picture). Ask your partner to describe the picture(s).

☐ EXERCISE 42. Paragraph practice.

> *Directions:* Choose one of the pictures your classmates brought to class. Describe the picture in a paragraph.

☐ EXERCISE 43. Chapter review.

> *Directions:* Circle the correct completions.

1. Jack lives _____ China.
   A. in   B. at   C. on

2. I need _____ a new notebook.
   A. buy   B. to buy   C. buying

3. "_____ a cup of tea?"
   "Yes, thank you."
   A. Would you like   B. Do you like   C. Are you like

4. There _____ twenty-two desks in this room.
   A. be   B. is   C. are

5. Pilots sit _____ an airplane.
   A. in front of   B. in the front of   C. front of

6. I live _____ 6601 Fourth Avenue.
   A. in   B. on   C. at

7. The students _____ do their homework.
   A. don't want   B. aren't wanting   C. don't want to

8. _____ a TV in Jane's bedroom?
   A. Are there   B. There   C. Is there

☐ EXERCISE 44. Chapter review: error analysis.

> *Directions:* Correct the errors.

1. Do you want go downtown with me?

2. There's many problems in big cities today.

3. I'd like see a movie tonight.

4. We are needing to find a new apartment soon.

5. Mr. Rice woulds likes to have a cup of tea.

6. How many students there are in your class?

7. Yoko and Ivan are study grammar right now. They want learn English.

8. I am like to leave now. How about you?

9. Please put the chair in middle the room.

10. The teacher needs to checking our homework now.

☐ EXERCISE 45. Review: Chapters 4 and 5.

Directions: Complete the sentences with your own words. Use your own paper.

1. I need _____ because _____.

2. I want _____ because _____.

3. I would like _____.

4. Would you like _____?

5. Do you like _____?

6. There is _____.

7. There are _____.

8. I'm listening to _____, but I also hear _____.

9. I'm looking at _____, but I also see _____.

10. I'm thinking about _____.

11. I think that _____.

12. In my opinion, _____.

13. How many _____ are there _____?

14. Is there _____?

15. Are there _____?

Directions: Complete the sentences. Use the words in parentheses. Use the simple present or the present progressive. Use an infinitive where necessary.

the baby = Bobby
the daughter = Ellen
the son = Paul
the mother = Mrs. Smith
the father = Mr. Smith
the cat = Puss
the bird = Tweetie
the mouse = Mickey

The Smiths are at home. It is evening. Paul *(sit)* _____ on
the sofa. He *(read)* _____ a newspaper. Ellen *(sit)*
                      2
_____ at the desk. She *(study)* _____.
           3   4
While she is studying, she *(listen to)* _____ music on her
                                                        5
radio. Paul *(hear)* _____ the music, but he *(listen to, not)*
                                    6
_____ it right now. He *(read)*
           7
_____ the weather report in the newspaper.
           8
    Ellen *(study)* _____ her chemistry text. She *(like)*
                                    9
_____ chemistry. She *(think)* _____ that chemistry is easy.
      10   11
She *(think about)* _____ chemical formulas. She
                                    12
(understand) _____ the formulas.
                      13
    Mrs. Smith is in the kitchen. She *(cook)* _____ dinner. She
                                                              14
(make) _____ a sauce for the pasta. Steam *(rise)* _____
                15   16

from the pot on the stove. Mrs. Smith *(like, not)* _____ 17 to

cook, but she *(know)* _____ 18 that her family has to eat good food. While

she *(make)* _____ 19 dinner, Mrs. Smith *(think about)*

_____ 20 a vacation on the beach. Sometimes Mrs.

Smith *(get)* _____ 21 tired of cooking all the time, but she *(love)*

_____ 22 her family very much and *(want)* _____ 23 to *(take)*

_____ 24 care of their health.

   Mr. Smith *(stand)* _____ 25 near the front door. He

(take off) _____ 26 his coat. Under his coat, he *(wear)*

_____ 27 a suit. Mr. Smith is happy to be home. He *(think about)*

_____ 28 dinner. After dinner, he *(want)*

_____ 29 *(watch)* _____ 30 television. He *(need)*

_____ 31 *(go)* _____ 32 to bed early tonight because he has a busy

day at work tomorrow.

   In the corner of the living room, a mouse *(eat)* _____ 33 a piece

of cheese. The mouse *(think)* _____ 34 that the cheese *(taste)*

_____ 35 good.

   Puss *(see, not)* _____ 36 the mouse. She *(smell, not)*

_____ 37 the mouse. Puss *(sleep)* _____ 38 .

She *(dream about)* _____ 39 a mouse.

   Bobby is in the middle of the living room. He *(play)* _____ 40

with a toy train. He *(see, not)* _____ 41 the mouse because he

(look at) _____ 42 his toy train. The bird, Tweetie, *(sing)*

_____ 43 . Bobby *(listen to, not)* _____ 44

the bird. He is busy with his train.

CHAPTER 6
Nouns and Pronouns

☐ **EXERCISE 1. Let's talk: small groups.**

Directions: Work in small groups. Name things that belong to each category. Make lists. Compare your lists with other groups' lists. All of the words you use in this exercise are called nouns.

1. Name clothing you see in this room. *(shirt)*
2. Name kinds of fruit. *(apple)*
3. Name things you drink. *(coffee)*
4. Name parts of the body. *(head)*
5. Name kinds of animals. *(horse)*
6. Name cities in the United States and Canada.★ *(New York, Montreal, etc.)*
7. Name languages.★ *(English)*
8. Name school subjects. *(history)*

6-1 NOUNS: SUBJECTS AND OBJECTS

NOUN (a) |**Birds**|fly.| subject verb	A NOUN is used as the **subject** of a sentence. A NOUN is used as the **object** of a verb.★ In (a): *Birds* is a NOUN. It is used as the subject of the sentence.
NOUN NOUN (b) |**John**|is holding|a **pen.**| subject verb object	In (b): *pen* is a NOUN. It has the article *a* in front of it; *a pen* is used as the object of the verb *is holding*.
NOUN NOUN (c) |**Birds**|fly|in|the **sky.**| subject verb prep. object of prep.	A NOUN is also used as the **object of a preposition.** In (c): *in* is a **preposition** (prep.). The noun *sky* (with the article *the* in front) is the OBJECT of the preposition *in*.
NOUN NOUN NOUN (d) |**John**|is holding|a **pen**|in|his **hand.**| subject verb object prep. object of prep.	Some common prepositions: *about, across, at, between, by, for, from, in, of, on, to, with.*

*Some verbs are followed by an object. These verbs are called transitive verbs (*v.t.* in a dictionary). Some verbs are not followed by an object. These verbs are called intransitive verbs (*v.i.* in a dictionary).

★ The names of cities and languages begin with capital letters.

158

☐ EXERCISE 2. Noun practice.

Directions: Check (✓) the words that are nouns.

1. _____ eat	7. _____ think
2. _____ dog	8. _____ mathematics
3. _____ beautiful	9. _____ flowers
4. _____ have	10. _____ juice
5. _____ eyes	11. _____ Paris
6. _____ English	12. _____ wonderful

☐ EXERCISE 3. Sentence practice.

Directions: Describe the grammatical structure of the sentences as shown in items 1 and 2. Then identify each noun. Is the noun used as

- the subject of the sentence?
- the object of the verb?
- the object of a preposition?

1. Marie studies chemistry.

Marie	*studies*	*chemistry*	*(none)*	*(none)*
subject	verb	object of verb	preposition	object of prep.

→ *Marie = a noun, subject of the sentence*
chemistry = a noun, object of the verb "studies"

2. The children are playing in the park.

The children	*are playing*	*(none)*	*in*	*the park*
subject	verb	object of verb	preposition	object of prep.

→ *children = a noun, subject of the sentence*
park = a noun, object of the preposition "in"

3. Children like candy.

subject	verb	object of verb	preposition	object of prep.

4. The teacher is erasing the board with her hand.

subject	verb	object of verb	preposition	object of prep.

5. Mike lives in Africa.

subject	verb	object of verb	preposition	object of prep.

6. The sun is shining.

subject	verb	object of verb	preposition	object of prep.

7. Robert is reading a book about butterflies.

subject	verb	object of verb	preposition	object of prep.

8. Tom and Ann live with their parents.

subject	verb	object of verb	preposition	object of prep.

9. Monkeys eat fruit and insects.

subject	verb	object of verb	preposition	object of prep.

10. Mary and Bob help Sue with her homework.

subject	verb	object of verb	preposition	object of prep.

11. Ships sail across the ocean.

subject	verb	object of verb	preposition	object of prep.

12. Water contains hydrogen and oxygen.

subject	verb	object of verb	preposition	object of prep.

6-2 ADJECTIVE + NOUN

(a) I don't like **cold** weather.
          adj. + noun
(b) Alex is a **happy** child.
          adj. + noun
(c) The **hungry** boy has a **fresh** apple.
    adj. + noun   adj. + noun
	An adjective (adj.) describes a noun. In grammar, we say that adjectives "modify" nouns. The word "modify" means "change a little." Adjectives give a little different meaning to a noun: *cold weather, hot weather, nice weather, bad weather.*
	Adjectives come in front of nouns.

(d) The *weather* *is* **cold**. noun + *be* + adj.	Reminder: An adjective can also follow **be**; the adjective describes the subject of the sentence. (See Chart 1-6, p. 12.)

COMMON ADJECTIVES

beautiful - ugly	good - bad	angry	hungry
big - little	happy - sad	bright	important
big - small	large - small	busy	intelligent
boring - interesting	long - short	delicious	kind
cheap - expensive	noisy - quiet	exciting	lazy
clean - dirty	old - new	famous	nervous
cold - hot	old - young	favorite	nice
dangerous - safe	poor - rich	free	nice
dry - wet	sour - sweet	fresh	ripe
easy - hard	strong - weak	healthy	serious
easy - difficult		honest	wonderful

☐ **EXERCISE 4. Sentence practice.**

Directions: Find the adjectives and nouns.

1. Jim has an expensive bicycle.
   → *Jim = a noun; expensive = an adjective; bicycle = a noun*

2. My sister has a beautiful house.

3. We often eat at an Italian restaurant.

4. Maria sings her favorite songs in the shower.

5. Olga likes American hamburgers.

6. You like sour apples, but I like sweet fruit.

7. Political leaders make important decisions.

8. Heavy traffic creates noisy streets.

9. Poverty causes serious problems in the world.

10. Young people have interesting ideas about modern music.

☐ EXERCISE 5. Let's talk: small groups.
Directions: Work in small groups. Take turns adding adjectives to the sentences. Use any adjectives that make sense. Think of at least three possible adjectives to complete each sentence.

1. I don't like ____*cold / hot / wet / rainy / bad / etc.*____ weather.

2. Do you like _____ food?

3. I admire _____ people.

4. _____ people make me angry.

5. Pollution is a/an _____ problem in the modern world.

6. I had a/an _____ experience yesterday.

7. I don't like _____ cities.

8. I had a/an _____ dinner last night.

☐ EXERCISE 6. Sentence practice.
Directions: Find each noun. Is the noun used as
  • the subject of the sentence?
  • the object of the verb?
  • the object of a preposition?

1. <u>Bob</u> and his <u>wife</u> like <u>coffee</u> with their <u>breakfast.</u>
  → *Bob = a noun, subject of the sentence*
     wife = a noun, subject of the sentence
     coffee = a noun, object of the verb "like"
     breakfast = a noun, object of the preposition "with"

2. Jack doesn't have a radio in his car.

3. Monkeys and apes have thumbs.

4. Does Janet work in a large office?

5. Scientists don't agree on the origin of the earth.

a chimpanzee

6. Egypt has hot summers and mild winters.

7. Many Vietnamese farmers live in small villages near their fields.

8. Large cities face many serious problems.

9. These problems include poverty, pollution, and crime.

10. An hour consists of 60 minutes. Does a day consist of 1440 minutes?

☐ EXERCISE 7. Let's talk: small groups.
Directions: Work in groups. When you are done, you will have a list of adjectives for different countries.

PART I. Complete each sentence with the name of a country and the appropriate adjective.

1. Food from _____*China*_____ is _____*Chinese*_____ food.

2. Food from _____*Mexico*_____ is _____ food.

3. Food from _____ is _____ food.

4. Food from _____ is _____ food.

5. Food from _____ is _____ food.

6. Food from _____ is _____ food.

7. Food from _____ is _____ food.

8. Food from _____ is _____ food.

PART II. What is the favorite ethnic food in your group? Give an example of this kind of food.

Example: Favorite ethnic food?
GROUP A: Italian
Example: An example of Italian food?
GROUP A: spaghetti

Favorite ethnic food in our group: _____

An example of this kind of food: _____

PART III. Find out the most popular ethnic food in other groups too.

PART IV. Working as a class, make a list of adjectives of nationality.

6-3 SUBJECT PRONOUNS AND OBJECT PRONOUNS

SUBJECT PRONOUNS	OBJECT PRONOUNS	SUBJECT	—	OBJECT
(a) *I* speak English.	(b) Bob knows *me*.	*I*	—	*me*
(c) *You* speak English.	(d) Bob knows *you*.	*you*	—	*you*
(e) *She* speaks English.	(f) Bob knows *her*.	*she*	—	*her*
(g) *He* speaks English.	(h) Bob knows *him*.	*he*	—	*him*
(i) *It* starts at 8:00.	(j) Bob knows *it*.	*it*	—	*it*
(k) *We* speak English.	(l) Bob talks to *us*.	*we*	—	*us*
(m) *You* speak English.	(n) Bob talks to *you*.	*you*	—	*you*
(o) *They* speak English.	(p) Bob talks to *them*.	*they*	—	*them*

(q) I know *Tony*. *He* is a friendly person.

(r) I like *Tony*. I know *him* well.

(s) I have *a red book*. *It* is on my desk.

A pronoun has the same meaning as a noun. In (q): *he* has the same meaning as *Tony*. In (r): *him* has the same meaning as *Tony*. In grammar, we say that a pronoun "refers to" a noun. The pronouns *he* and *him* refer to the noun *Tony*.

Sometimes a pronoun refers to a "noun phrase." In (s): *it* refers to the whole phrase *a red book*.

□ EXERCISE 8. Sentence practice.

Directions: Complete the sentences. Use pronouns *(I, me, he, him, etc.)*.

1. John loves Mary. _____*He*_____ loves _____*her*_____ very much.

2. Mary loves John. _____ loves _____ very much.

3. Mary and John love their daughter, Anna. _____ love _____ very much.

4. Mary and John love their son, Tom. _____ love _____ very much.

5. Tom loves his little sister, Anna. _____ loves _____ very much.

6. Mary loves her children. _____ loves _____ very much.

7. John loves his children. _____ loves _____ very much.

8. Mary and John love Tom and Anna. _____ love _____ very much.

☐ **EXERCISE 9. Sentence practice.**

    Directions: Complete the sentences. Use pronouns (***I, me, he, him,*** *etc.*).

1. Rita has a book. _____*She*_____ bought _____*it*_____ last week.

2. I know the new students, but Tony doesn't know _____ yet.

3. I wrote a letter, but I can't send _____ because I don't have a stamp.

4. Tom is in Canada. _____ is studying at a university.

5. Bill lives in my dorm. I eat breakfast with _____ every morning.

6. Ann is my neighbor. I talk to _____ every day. _____ and
       _____ have interesting conversations.

7. I have two pictures on my bedroom wall. I like _____. _____
       are beautiful.

8. Ann and I have a dinner invitation. Mr. and Mrs. Brown want _____ to
       come to dinner at their house.

9. Judy has a new car. _____ is a Toyota.

10. My husband and I have a new car. _____ got _____ last month.

☐ **EXERCISE 10. Let's talk: find someone who . . . .**

    Directions: Interview your classmates. Find someone who can answer *yes* to a
question. Then ask the follow-up question using the appropriate object pronoun.

Example:
SPEAKER A: Do you send e-mails?
SPEAKER B: No, I don't.
SPEAKER A: *(Ask another student.)* Do you send e-mails?
SPEAKER C: Yes, I do.
SPEAKER A: When do you send **them**?
SPEAKER C: I send **them** in the evenings.

1. Do you do your homework?
   When do you . . . ?
2. Do you visit friends?
   When do you . . . ?
3. Do you read newspapers or magazines?
   When do you . . . ?
4. Do you talk to *(name of female classmate)*?
   When do you . . . ?

5. Do you watch TV?
   When do you . . . ?
6. Do you buy groceries?
   When do you . . . ?
7. Do you wear boots?
   When do you . . . ?
8. Do you use a computer?
   When do you . . . ?

□ EXERCISE 11. Sentence practice.

    Directions: Complete the sentences. Use pronouns.

1. A: Do you know Kate and Jim?

   B: Yes, _____*I*_____ do. I live near _____*them*_____.

2. A: Is the chemical formula for water H_3O?

   B: No, _____ isn't. _____ is H_2O.

3. A: Would Judy and you like to come to the movie with us?

   B: Yes, _____ would. Judy and _____ would enjoy going to

   the movie with _____.

4. A: Do Mr. and Mrs. Kelly live in the city?

   B: No, _____ don't. _____ live in the suburbs. I visited

   _____ last month.

5. A: Do you know how to spell "Mississippi"?

   B: Sure! I can spell _____. _____ is easy to spell.

6. A: Is Paul Cook in your class?

   B: Yes, _____ is. I sit next to _____.

□ EXERCISE 12. Listening practice.

    Directions: Listen to the sentences. Note that the "h" in ***her*** and ***him*** is often dropped in spoken English. The "th" in ***them*** can also be dropped. Discuss the pronunciation changes.

1. Sara knows Joe. She knows him very well.
2. Where does Shelley live? Do you have her address?
3. There's Sam. Let's go talk to him.
4. There're Bill and Julie. Let's go talk to them.
5. The teacher is speaking with Lisa because she doesn't have her homework.
6. I need to see our airline tickets. Do you have them?

☐ EXERCISE 13. Listening.

Directions: Listen to each conversation and complete the sentences.

Example:

You will hear: How is Mr. Adams doing?

You will write: How _____*is*_____ Mr. Adams doing?

You will hear: Great! I see him every week at the office.

You will write: Great! I see _____*him*_____ every week at the office.

1. A: Yoko and _____ downtown this afternoon. Do

   you want to come _____?

  B: I don't think so, but thanks anyway. Chris and _____

   to the library. _____ study for our test.

2. A: Hi, Ann. How do you like your new apartment?

  B: _____ very nice.

  A: Do you have a roommate?

  B: Yes. Maria Hall is my roommate. Do you _____?

  _____ Miami.

  A: No, I don't _____. Do you get along _____?

  B: Yes, _____ living together. You must _____

  _____ sometime. Maybe _____ can come over for

  dinner soon.

  A: Thanks. _____ that.

3. A: Do George and Mike come over to your house often?

  B: Yes, _____. I invite _____
   to my house often. We like to play cards.

  A: Who usually wins your card games?

  B: Mike. _____ a really good
   card player. We can't beat

  _____.

6-4 NOUNS: SINGULAR AND PLURAL

	SINGULAR	PLURAL		
(a)	*one pen* *one apple* *one cup* *one elephant*	*two pens* *three apples* *four cups* *five elephants*	To make the plural form of most nouns, add **-s**.	
(b)	*baby* *city*	*babies* *cities*	End of noun: Plural form:	*consonant* + **-y** change *y* to *i*, add **-es**.
(c)	*boy* *key*	*boys* *keys*	End of noun: Plural form:	*vowel* + **-y** add **-s**.
(d)	*wife* *thief*	*wives* *thieves*	End of noun: Plural form:	**-fe** or **-f** change *f* to *v*, add **-es**.
(e)	*dish* *match* *class* *box*	*dishes* *matches* *classes* *boxes*	End of noun: Plural form: Pronunciation:	**-sh, -ch, -ss, -x** add **-es**. /əz/
(f)	*tomato* *potato* *zoo* *radio*	*tomatoes* *potatoes* *zoos* *radios*	End of noun: Plural form: End of noun: Plural form:	*consonant* + **-o** add **-es**. *vowel* + **-o** add **-s**.

☐ EXERCISE 14. Sentence practice.

Directions: Complete the sentences. Use the plural form of the words in the lists. Use each word only once.

LIST A.

baby	cowboy	lady
✓ boy	dictionary	party
city	key	tray
country		

1. Mr. and Mrs. Parker have one daughter and two sons. They have one girl and two ___boys___ .

2. The students in my class come from many _____.

3. Women give birth to _____.

4. My money and my _____ are in my pocket.

5. I know the names of many _____ in the United States and Canada.

6. I like to go to _____ because I like to meet and talk to people.

7. People carry their food on _____ in a cafeteria.

8. We always use our _____ when we write compositions.

9. Good evening, _____ and gentlemen.

10. _____ ride horses.

LIST B.

knife	life	wife
leaf	thief	

11. It is fall. The _____ are falling from the trees.

12. Sue and Ann are married. They have husbands.

They are _____.

13. We all have some problems in our _____.

14. Police officers catch _____.

15. Please put the _____, forks, and spoons

on the table.

LIST C.

bush	glass	sandwich	tomato
class	match	sex	zoo
dish	potato	tax	

16. Bob drinks eight _____ of water every day.

17. There are two _____: male and female.

18. Please put the _____ and the silverware on the table.

19. All citizens pay money to the government every year. They pay their

_____.

20. I can see trees and _____ outside the window.

21. I want to light the candles. I need some _____.

22. When I make a salad, I use lettuce and _____.

23. Sometimes Sue has a hamburger and French-fried

_____ for dinner.

24. We often eat _____ for lunch.

25. Mehmet is a student. He likes his _____.

26. Some animals live all of their lives in _____.

☐ EXERCISE 15. Pronunciation practice.

Directions: Listen to the pronunciation of final **-s/-es**. Practice saying the words.

GROUP A. Final **-s** is pronounced /z/ after voiced sounds.*

1. taxicabs
2. beds
3. dogs
4. balls
5. rooms
6. coins
7. years
8. lives
9. trees
10. cities
11. boys
12. days

_____

* For more information on voiced sounds, see Chart 3-8, p. 66.

GROUP B. Final *-s* is pronounced /s/ after voiceless sounds.★

13. books   16. groups
14. desks   17. cats
15. cups   18. students

GROUP C. Final *-s/-es* is pronounced /əz/.

• after "s" sounds:	19. classes
	20. glasses
	21. horses
	22. places
	23. sentences
• after "z" sounds:	24. sizes
	25. exercises
	26. noises
• after "sh" sounds:	27. dishes
	28. bushes
• after "ch" sounds:	29. matches
	30. sandwiches
• after "ge/dge" sounds:	31. pages
	32. oranges
	33. bridges

☐ EXERCISE 16. Listening.

 Directions: Listen to each word. Circle the noun you hear.

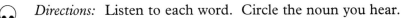

1. toy   (toys)
2. table   tables
3. face   faces
4. hat   hats
5. office   offices
6. box   boxes
7. package   packages
8. chair   chairs
9. edge   edges
10. top   tops

_____

★ For more information on voiceless sounds, see Chart 3-8, p. 66.

☐ EXERCISE 17. Listening.

○○ *Directions:* Listen to each sentence. Circle the noun you hear.

1. desk (desks)
2. place places
3. sandwich sandwiches
4. sentence sentences
5. apple apples

6. exercise exercises
7. piece pieces
8. rose roses
9. bush bushes
10. college colleges

☐ EXERCISE 18. Pronunciation practice.

Directions: Find the plural noun(s) in each sentence. Pronounce the noun(s). Then read the sentences aloud.

1. The students are carrying books and backpacks.

2. Department stores sell many sizes of clothes.

3. The weather is terrible. It's raining cats and dogs.*

4. The teachers have their offices in this building.

5. Engineers build bridges.

6. At the zoo you can see tigers, monkeys, birds, elephants, bears, and snakes.

7. People have two ears, two eyes, two arms, two hands, two legs, and two feet.

8. Square tables and rectangular tables have four edges.

9. My dictionary has 350 pages.

10. I like apples, bananas, strawberries, and peaches.

11. My apartment has cockroaches in the kitchen.

---

*The idiom "raining cats and dogs" means "raining very hard."

SINGULAR	PLURAL	EXAMPLES
(a) *child*	**children**	Mr. Smith has one *child*. Mr. Cook has two **children**.
(b) *foot*	**feet**	I have a right *foot* and a left *foot*. I have two **feet**.
(c) *man*	**men**	I see a *man* on the street. I see two **men** on the street.
(d) *mouse*	**mice**	My cat sees a *mouse*. Cats like to catch **mice**.
(e) *tooth*	**teeth**	My *tooth* hurts. My **teeth** are white.
(f) *woman*	**women**	There's one *woman* in our class. There are ten **women** in your class.
(g) *sheep*	**sheep**	Annie drew a picture of one *sheep*. Tommy drew a picture of two **sheep**.
		one sheep two sheep
(h) *fish*	**fish**	Bob has an aquarium. He has one *fish*. Sue has an aquarium. She has seven **fish**.
		seven fish one fish
(h) *(none)*★	**people**	There are fifteen **people** in this room. (Notice: *People* does not have a final *-s*.)

★***People*** is always plural. It has no singular form.

☐ EXERCISE 19. Game.

Directions: Work in groups or individually. The object of the game on p. 174 is to fill in each list with nouns. If possible, write one noun that begins with each letter of the alphabet. The nouns must belong to the category of the list. When you finish your lists, count the number of nouns you have. That is your score. Who has the highest score?

	List 1 Things in nature	List 2 Things you eat and drink	List 3 Animals and insects	List 4 Things for sale at *(name of a local store)*
A	*air*			
B	*bushes*			
C				
D				
E	*earth*			
F	*fish*			
G	*grass*			
H				
I	*ice*			
J				
K				
L	*leaves*			
M				
N				
O	*ocean*			
P	*plants*			
Q				
R	*rain*			
S	*stars*			
T	*trees*			
U				
V				
W	*water*			
X				
Y				
Z				
	Score: ___13___	Score: _____	Score: _____	Score: _____

□ EXERCISE 20. Let's talk: class activity.

Directions: Your teacher will say a noun. You say the plural form with ***two***. Close your books for this activity.

Example:
TEACHER: one child
STUDENTS: two children

1. one child
2. one woman
3. one tooth
4. one foot
5. one man
6. one mouse
7. one fish
8. one page
9. one place
10. one banana
11. one child
12. one desk
13. one sentence
14. one man
15. one orange
16. one foot
17. one knife
18. one sex
19. one girl
20. one exercise
21. one tooth
22. one woman
23. one boy and one woman

□ EXERCISE 21. Review.

Directions: Fill in the grammatical structure of the sentences. Item 1 has been completed for you.

1. Mr. Cook is living in a hotel.

Mr. Cook	is living	(none)	in	a hotel
subject	verb	object	preposition	object of prep.

2. Anita carries her books in her backpack.

subject	verb	object	preposition	object of prep.

3. Snow falls.

subject	verb	object	preposition	object of prep.

4. Monkeys sleep in trees.

subject	verb	object	preposition	object of prep.

5. The teacher is writing words on the chalkboard.

| subject | verb | object | preposition | object of prep. |

6. I like apples.

| subject | verb | object | preposition | object of prep. |

☐ EXERCISE 22.   Review.

Directions: A *complete sentence* has a subject and a verb. An *incomplete sentence* is a group of words that does not have a subject and a verb.

If the words are a complete sentence, change the first letter to a capital letter (a big letter) and add final punctuation (a period or a question mark). If the words are an incomplete sentence, write "*Inc.*" to mean "*Incomplete.*"

1. monkeys like bananas → **M**/onkeys like bananas.

2. in my garden → *Inc.*

3. do you like sour apples → **D**/o you like sour apples?

4. this class ends at two o'clock

5. teaches English

6. my mother works

7. in an office

8. my mother works in an office

9. does your brother have a job

10. does not work

11. rain falls

12. my sister lives in an apartment

13. has a roommate

14. the apartment has two bedrooms

15. a small kitchen and a big living room

16. on the third floor

☐ EXERCISE 23. Review.
   Directions: Circle the correct completions.

1. My sister and I live together. Our parents often call _____ on the telephone.
   A. us   B. them   C. we   D. they

2. Tom has a broken leg. I visit _____ every day.
   A. he   B. him   C. them   D. it

3. Sue and I are good friends. _____ spend a lot of time together.
   A. They   B. You   C. We   D. She

4. Our children enjoy the zoo. We often take _____ to the zoo.
   A. it   B. they   C. them   D. him

5. Mary drives an old car. She takes good care of _____.
   A. her   B. them   C. it   D. him

6. Jack and _____ don't know Mr. Wu.
   A. I   B. me   C. us   D. them

7. Ms. Gray is a lawyer in Chicago. Do you know _____?
   A. them   B. it   C. him   D. her

8. Ahmed lives near Yoko and _____.
   A. I   B. me   C. him   D. her

9. My sister and a friend are visiting me. _____ are visiting here for two days.
   A. She   B. They   C. We   D. Them

10. Do _____ have the correct time?
   A. you   B. them   C. him   D. her

□ **EXERCISE 24. Chapter review: error analysis.**

Directions: Correct the errors.

1. Omar a car has. → *Omar has a car.*

2. Our teacher gives tests difficult.

3. Alex helps Mike and I.

4. Babys cry.

5. Mike and Tom in an apartment live.

6. There are seven woman in this class.

7. There are nineteen peoples in my class.

8. Olga and Ivan has three childrens.

9. There is twenty classroom in this building.

10. Mr. Jones is our teacher. I like her very much.

CHAPTER 7
Count and Noncount Nouns

☐ EXERCISE 1. Preview: noun practice.

Directions: Describe the pictures. Add **-s** to the ends of the words if necessary. Otherwise, write an "x."

Picture	Description
	1. one ring ___x___
	2. two ring __s___
	3. three ring __s___
	4. some jewelry ___x___
	5. two letter _____
	6. one postcard _____
	7. some mail _____

Picture	Description
	8. one sofa _____
	9. two table _____
	10. some chair _____
	11. some furniture _____
	12. a lot of car _____
	13. a lot of traffic _____
	14. a lot of money _____
	15. a lot of coin _____

7-1 NOUNS: COUNT AND NONCOUNT

	SINGULAR	PLURAL	
COUNT NOUN	*a book* *one book*	*books* *two books* *some books* *a lot of books*	**A COUNT NOUN** SINGULAR: *a* + *noun* *one* + *noun* PLURAL: *noun* + *-s*
NONCOUNT NOUN	*mail* *some mail* *a lot of mail*	(no plural form)	**A NONCOUNT NOUN** SINGULAR: Do not use *a*. Do not use *one*. PLURAL: A noncount noun does not have a plural form.

COMMON NONCOUNT NOUNS

advice	*mail*	*bread*	*pepper*
furniture	*money*	*cheese*	*rice*
help	*music*	*coffee*	*salt*
homework	*traffic*	*food*	*soup*
information	*vocabulary*	*fruit*	*sugar*
jewelry	*weather*	*meat*	*tea*
luck	*work*	*milk*	*water*

☐ EXERCISE 2. Noun practice.

Directions: Look at the *italicized* words. <u>Underline</u> the noun. Is it count or noncount?

1. He sits on *a <u>chair</u>*.   (count)   noncount

2. He sits on *<u>furniture</u>*.   count   (noncount)

3. She has *a coin*.   count   noncount

4. She has *some money*.   count   noncount

5. The street is full of *traffic*.   count   noncount

6. There are *a lot of cars* in the street.   count   noncount

7. I know *a fact* about bees.   count   noncount

8. I have *some information* about bees.   count   noncount

9. The teacher gives us *homework*.   count   noncount

10. We have *an assignment*.   count   noncount

11. I like *music*.   count   noncount

12. Would you like *some coffee*?   count   noncount

13. Our school has *a library*.   count   noncount

14. We are learning new *vocabulary* every day.   count   noncount

15. I need *some advice*.   count   noncount

16. Tom has *a good job*.   count   noncount

17. He likes *his work*.   count   noncount

18. Maria wears *a lot of bracelets*.   count   noncount

☐ EXERCISE 3. Let's talk: small groups.

Directions: Work in small groups. List the noncount nouns. Then find the count nouns that are close in meaning. Use *a/an* with the count nouns.

advice	*furniture*	*money*
assignment	*homework*	*music*
bracelet	*information*	*song*
cloud	*jewelry*	*suggestion*
coin	*job*	*weather*
desk	✓ *letter*	*work*
fact	✓ *mail*	

	NONCOUNT	COUNT
1.	*mail*	*a letter*
2.		
3.		
4.		
5.		
6.		
7.		
8.		
9.		
10.		

☐ EXERCISE 4. Let's talk: class activity.

Directions: Most nouns are count nouns. Complete the sentences by naming things you see in the classroom.

1. I see a . . . .

2. I see a . . . .

3. I see a . . . . and a . . . .

4. I see two . . . .

5. I see five . . . .

6. I see some . . . .

7. I see a lot of . . . .

8. I see many . . . .

7-2 USING *AN* vs. *A*

(a) *A* dog is *an* animal.	*A* and *an* are used in front of singular count nouns. In (a): *dog* and *animal* are singular count nouns.
(b) I work in *an* office. (c) Mr. Lee is *an* old man.	Use *an* in front of words that begin with the vowels *a, e, i,* and *o: an apartment, an elephant, an idea, an ocean.* In (c): Notice that *an* is used because the adjective *(old)* begins with a vowel and comes in front of a singular count noun *(man).*
(d) I have *an* uncle. COMPARE (e) He works at *a* university.	Use *an* if a word that begins with "*u*" has a vowel sound: *an uncle, an ugly picture.* Use *a* if a word that begins with "*u*" has a /yu/ sound: *a university, a usual event.*
(f) I need *an* hour to finish my work. COMPARE (g) I live in *a* house. He lives in *a* hotel.	In some words that begin with "*h*," the "*h*" is not pronounced. Instead, the word begins with a vowel sound and *an* is used: *an hour, an honor.* In most words that begin with "*h*," the "*h*" is pronounced. Use *a* if the "*h*" is pronounced.

☐ EXERCISE 5. Sentence practice.

Directions: Complete the sentences. Use *a* or *an.*

1. Bob is eating _____ apple.

2. Tom is eating _____ banana.

3. Alice works in _____ office.

4. I have _____ idea.

5. I have _____ good idea.

6. Sue is taking _____ class.

7. Sue is taking _____ easy class.

8. Cuba is _____ island near the United States.

9. _____ hour has sixty minutes.

10. _____ healthy person gets regular exercise.

11. _____ horse has a long nose.

12. Maria is _____ honest worker.

13. Mark needs _____ math tutor.

14. _____ university is _____ educational institution.

15. Ann has _____ unusual job.

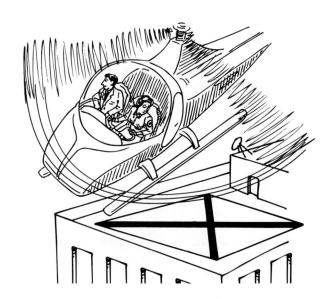

□ EXERCISE 6. Listening.

Directions: Listen to each sentence. Circle the word you hear.

1. a	(an)		6. a	an
2. a	an		7. a	an
3. a	an		8. a	an
4. a	an		9. a	an
5. a	an		10. a	an

7-3 USING A/AN vs. SOME

(a) I have **a** pen. (b) I have **some** pens.	**A/An** is used in front of **singular** count nouns. In (a): The word *pen* is a singular count noun. **Some** is used in front of **plural** count nouns. In (b): The word *pens* is a plural count noun.
(c) I have **some** rice.	**Some** is used in front of noncount nouns.* In (c): The word *rice* is a noncount noun.

*Reminder: Noncount nouns do not have a plural form. Noncount nouns are grammatically singular.

☐ EXERCISE 7. Noun practice.

Directions: Look at the noun and circle the correct word *(a, an,* or *some)*. Then decide if the noun is singular count, plural count, or noncount.

					sing. count	pl. count	noncount
1.	a	an	(some)	letters		✓	
2.	a	an	(some)	mail			✓
3.	(a)	an	some	letter	✓		
4.	a	an	some	table			
5.	a	an	some	tables			
6.	a	an	some	furniture			
7.	a	an	some	car			
8.	a	an	some	automobiles			
9.	a	an	some	buses			
10.	a	an	some	traffic			
11.	a	an	some	advice			
12.	a	an	some	egg			

☐ EXERCISE 8. Sentence practice.

Directions: Use *a/an* or *some* with the count nouns in these sentences. Are the nouns singular or plural?

1. Bob has _____*a*_____ book on his desk. → *book = a singular count noun*

2. Bob has _____*some*_____ books on his desk. → *books = a plural count noun*

3. I see _____ desk in this room.

4. I see _____ desks in this room.

5. I'm hungry. I would like _____ apple.

6. The children are hungry. They would like _____ apples.

7. We are doing _____ exercise in class.

8. We are doing _____ exercises in class.

☐ EXERCISE 9. Sentence practice.
   Directions: Use *a, an,* or *some* with the nouns in these sentences. Are they singular count nouns or noncount nouns?

   1. I need _____*some*_____ money. → *money = a noncount noun*

   2. I need _____*a*_____ dollar. → *dollar = a singular count noun*

   3. Alice has _____ mail in her mailbox.

   4. Alice has _____ letter in her mailbox.

   5. I'm hungry. I would like _____ fruit.

   6. I would like _____ apple.

   7. Jane is hungry. She would like _____ food.

   8. She would like _____ sandwich.

   9. I'd like to have _____ soup with my sandwich.

   10. I'm thirsty. I'd like _____ water.

☐ EXERCISE 10. Let's talk: small groups.
   Directions: Work in small groups. Complete the lists with nouns. You may use adjectives with the nouns. Share some of your answers with the class.

   1. Things you can see in an apartment.

      a _____

      an _____

      some _____ (plural noun)

      some _____ (singular noun)

186 CHAPTER 7

2. Things you can see in a classroom.

a _____

an _____

some _____ (plural noun)

some _____ (singular noun)

3. Things you can see outdoors.

a _____

an _____

some _____ (plural noun)

some _____ (singular noun)

☐ EXERCISE 11. Sentence practice.
   Directions: Use ***a/an*** or ***some*** with the nouns in these sentences.

1. Sonya is wearing _____*some*_____ silver jewelry. She's wearing

   _____*a*_____ necklace and _____*some*_____ earrings.

2. I'm busy. I have _____ homework to do.

3. Jane is very busy. She has _____ work to do.

4. Jane has _____ job. She is _____ teacher.

5. We have _____ table, _____ sofa, and _____ chairs in

   our living room.

6. We have _____ furniture in our living room.

7. Susan has a CD player. She is listening to _____ music.

8. I'm hungry. I would like _____ orange.

9. The children are hungry. They would like _____ oranges. They would

   like _____ fruit.

10. I need _____ information about the bus schedule.

11. I'm confused. I need _____ advice.

12. I'm looking out the window. I see _____ cars, _____ bus, and

_____ trucks on the street. I see _____ traffic.

☐ EXERCISE 12. Let's talk: pairwork.
   Directions: Work with a partner.
   Partner A: Your book is open to this page. Use *a, an,* or *some* with the given word.
   Partner B: Your book is open to p. 515. Help Partner A with the correct response if
       necessary.

Example: desk
PARTNER A: a desk
PARTNER B: Right.

Example: desks
PARTNER A: a desks
PARTNER B: Again?
PARTNER A: some desks
PARTNER B: Right.

1. apple	6. flower	11. rice
2. apples	7. man	12. advice
3. child	8. old man	13. hour
4. children	9. men	14. horse
5. music	10. island	15. food

Switch roles.
Partner B: Your book is open to this page. Use *a, an,* or *some* with the given word.
Partner A: Your book is open to p. 515. Help Partner B with the correct response if
       necessary.

16. animal	21. homework	26. university
17. animals	22. orange	27. uncle
18. chair	23. bananas	28. people
19. chairs	24. banana	29. house
20. furniture	25. fruit	30. bread

☐ **EXERCISE 13. Sentence practice.**

Directions: Use the word in *italics* to complete the sentence. Add **-s** to a count noun (or give the irregular plural form). Do not add **-s** to a noncount noun.

1. *money*   I need some _____money_____.

2. *desk*   I see some _____desks_____ in this room.

3. *man*   Some _____men_____ are working in the street.

4. *music*   I want to listen to some _____.

5. *flower*   Andy wants to buy some _____ for his girlfriend.

6. *information* I need some _____.

7. *jewelry*   Fred wants to buy some _____.

8. *child*   Some _____ are playing in the park.

9. *homework*   I can't go to the movie because I have some _____ to do.

10. *advice*   Could you please give me some _____?

11. *suggestion* I have some _____ for you.

12. *help*   I need some _____ with my homework.

13. *sandwich* We're hungry. We want to make some _____.

14. *animal*   I see some _____ in the picture.

15. *banana*   The monkeys are hungry. They would like some _____.

16. *fruit*   I'm hungry. I would like some _____.

17. *weather*   We're having some hot _____ right now.

18. *picture*   I have some _____ of my family in my wallet.

19. *rice, bean* I usually have some _____ and

                           _____ for dinner.

☐ EXERCISE 14. Sentence practice.

    Directions: Change the *italicized* noun to its plural form if possible, changing **a** to **some**. Make other changes in the sentence as necessary.

1. There is *a chair* in this room. PLURAL FORM → *There are some chairs in this room.*

2. There is *some furniture* in this room. PLURAL FORM → *(none)*

3. I have *a coin* in my pocket.

4. I have *some money* in my wallet.

5. There's *a lot of traffic* on Main Street.

6. There's *a car* on Main Street.

7. Our teacher assigns *a lot of homework*.

8. I like rock *music*.

9. Hong Kong has *a lot of hot weather*.

10. I need *some information* and *some advice* from you.

11. There's *a dictionary* on the shelf.

12. I hope you do well on your exam. Good *luck!*

13. Here is *a flower* from my garden.

14. Be careful! There's *some water* on the floor.

15. I need *an apple* for the fruit salad.

16. The soup needs *a potato* and *some salt*.

7-4 MEASUREMENTS WITH NONCOUNT NOUNS

(a) I'd like **some** water.	Units of measure are used with noncount nouns to express a specific quantity. For example: *a glass of, a cup of, a piece of.*
(b) I'd like **a glass of** water.	In (a): *some water* = an unspecific quantity.
(c) I'd like **a cup of** coffee.	In (b): *a glass of water* = a specific quantity.
(d) I'd like **a piece of** fruit.	

COMMON EXPRESSIONS OF MEASURE

a bag of rice	a bunch of bananas	a jar of pickles
a bar of soap	a can of corn★	a loaf of bread
a bottle of olive oil	a carton of milk	a piece of cheese
a bowl of cereal	a glass of water	a sheet of paper
a box of candy	a head of lettuce	a tube of toothpaste

bag   bar   bottle   box

can   carton   jar   tube   bunch

★In British English: *a tin of corn.*

☐ **EXERCISE 15. Noun practice.**

Directions: Complete the phrases. You are hungry and thirsty. What would you like? Use *a piece of, a cup of, a glass of, a bowl of.*

1. _____*a cup of / a glass of*_____ tea

2. _____ bread

3. _____ water

4. _____ coffee

5. _____ cheese

6. _____ soup

7. _____ meat

8. _____ wine

9. _____ fruit

10. _____ rice

☐ EXERCISE 16. Let's talk: pairwork.
> *Directions:* Work in pairs. Look at the list of food and drink. Check (✓) what you eat and drink every day. Add your own words to the list. Then tell your partner the usual <u>quantity</u> you have every day. Use ***a piece of, two pieces of, a cup of, three cups of, a glass of, a bowl of,*** or ***one, two, a, some,*** etc., in your answers. Share a few of your partner's answers with the class.
>
> *Example:*
> __✓__ egg
> _____ banana
> _____ coffee
> __✓__ fruit
> _____ *ice cream*
> _____ *orange juice*
>
> PARTNER A: I have one egg every day.
> I usually eat two pieces of fruit.
> I like a bowl of ice cream at night.
> I drink a glass of orange juice every morning.
>
> *List of food and drinks.*
>
> | | | | |
> |---|---|---|---|
> | _____ egg | | _____ rice | |
> | _____ soup | | _____ ice cream | |
> | _____ fruit | | _____ water | |
> | _____ bread | | _____ chicken | |
> | _____ banana | | _____ cheese | |
> | _____ apples | | _____ tea | |
>
> _____   _____
>
> _____   _____
>
> _____   _____

☐ EXERCISE 17. Sentence practice.
> *Directions:* Complete the sentences with nouns.
>
> 1. I'm going to the store. I need to buy a carton of __*orange juice / milk / etc.*__
>
> 2. I also need a tube of _____ and two bars of
>
> _____ .

3. I need to find a can of _____ and a jar of _____.

4. I need to get a loaf of _____ and a box of _____.

5. I would like a head of _____ if it looks fresh.

6. Finally, I would like a couple of bottles of _____ and a jar of _____.

□ EXERCISE 18. Review.

Directions: Make a list of everything in the picture by completing the sentence **I see .... .** Try to use numbers (e.g., **three** *spoons*) or other units of measure (e.g., **a box of** *candy*). Use **a** for singular count nouns (e.g., **a** *fly*).

Example: I see three spoons, a box of candy, a fly, etc.

□ EXERCISE 19. Review: pairwork.

Directions: Work in pairs. Pretend that tomorrow you are moving into a new apartment together. What do you need? Ask each other questions.

In writing, list the things you need and indicate quantity (**two**, **some**, **a lot of**, **a little**, *etc.*). List twenty to thirty things. Be sure to write down the <u>quantity</u>. You are completing this sentence: **We need .... .**

Example: We need . . .
PARTNER A: a sofa and two beds.
PARTNER B: a can opener.
PARTNER A: some spaghetti.
PARTNER B: a little fruit.
PARTNER A: some bookcases.
Etc.

☐ EXERCISE 20. Let's talk: pairwork.

Directions: Work with a partner.

Partner A: Your book is open to this page. Complete the sentences by using *a, an,* or *some* with the nouns.

Partner B: Your book is open to p. 515. Help Partner A with the correct responses if necessary.

1. I'm hungry. I'd like . . .
   a. food.
   b. apple.
   c. sandwich.
   d. bowl of soup.

2. I'm thirsty. I'd like . . .
   a. glass of milk.
   b. water.
   c. cup of tea.

3. I'm sick. I need . . .
   a. medicine.
   b. ambulance.

4. I'm cold. I need . . .
   a. coat.
   b. hat.
   c. warm clothes.
   d. heat.

5. I'm tired. I need . . .
   a. sleep.
   b. break.
   c. relaxing vacation.

Switch roles.

Partner B: Your book is open to this page. Complete the sentences by using *a, an,* or *some* with the nouns.

Partner A: Your book is open to p. 515. Help Partner B with the correct responses if necessary.

6. I'm hungry. I'd like . . .
   a. snack.
   b. fruit.
   c. orange.
   d. piece of chicken.

7. I'm thirsty. I'd like . . .
   a. juice.
   b. bottle of water.
   c. glass of ice tea.

8. I'm sick. I need . . .
   a. doctor.
   b. help.

9. I'm cold. I need . . .
   a. boots.
   b. blanket.
   c. hot bath.
   d. gloves.

10. I'm tired. I need . . .
    a. strong coffee.
    b. break.
    c. vacation.
    d. nap.

7-5 USING *MANY, MUCH, A FEW, A LITTLE*

(a) I don't get *many* letters.	In (a): *many* is used with PLURAL COUNT nouns.
(b) I don't get *much* mail.	In (b): *much* is used with NONCOUNT nouns.
(c) Ann gets *a few* letters.	In (c): *a few* is used with PLURAL COUNT nouns.
(d) Tom gets *a little* mail.	In (d): *a little* is used with NONCOUNT nouns.

☐ EXERCISE 21. Sentence practice.

Directions: Change *a lot of* to *many* or *much* in these sentences.

1. Tom has a lot of problems. → *Tom has many problems.*

2. I don't have a lot of money. → *I don't have much money.*

3. I want to visit a lot of cities in the United States and Canada.

4. I don't put a lot of sugar in my coffee.

5. I have a lot of questions to ask you.

6. Sue and John have a small apartment. They don't have a lot of furniture.

7. You can see a lot of people at the zoo on Sunday.

8. Dick doesn't get a lot of mail because he doesn't write a lot of letters.

9. Chicago has a lot of skyscrapers. Montreal has a lot of tall buildings too.

10. Mary is lazy. She doesn't do a lot of work.

11. I don't drink a lot of coffee.

12. Jeff is a friendly person. He has a lot of friends.

13. Do you usually buy a lot of fruit at the market?

14. Does Andy drink a lot of coffee?

15. Do you write a lot of letters?

☐ EXERCISE 22. Sentence practice.

Directions: Complete the questions with *many* or *much*.

1. How _____*much*_____ money do you have in your wallet?

2. How _____*many*_____ roommates do you have?

3. How _____ languages do you speak?

4. How _____ homework does your teacher usually assign?

5. How _____ tea do you drink in a day?

6. How _____ sugar do you put in your tea?

7. How _____ sentences are there in this exercise?

8. How _____ water do you need to cook rice?

☐ EXERCISE 23. Let's talk: pairwork.

Directions: Work with a partner.

Partner A: Your book is open to this page. Make questions with **how many** or **how much** and **are there** or **is there**.

Partner B: Help Partner A if necessary.

Example: students in this room
PARTNER A: How many students is there in this room?
PARTNER B: Please try again.
PARTNER A: How many students are there in this room?
PARTNER B: Right.

Example: coffee in that pot
PARTNER A: How much coffee is there in that pot?
PARTNER B: Right.

1. restaurants in *(name of this city)*
2. desks in this room
3. furniture in this room
4. letters in your mailbox today
5. mail in your mailbox today

Switch roles.

Partner B: Your book is open to this page. Make questions with **how many** or **how much** and **are there** or **is there**.

Partner A: Help Partner B if necessary.

6. chicken in your refrigerator
7. bridges in *(name of this city)*
8. traffic on the street right now
9. cars in the street outside the window
10. people in this room

□ EXERCISE 24. Sentence practice.

   Directions: Change **some** to **a few** or **a little**. Use **a few** with count nouns. Use **a little** with noncount nouns. (See Chart 7-5, p. 195.)

   1. I need some paper. → *I need a little paper.*

   2. I usually add some salt to my food.

   3. I have some questions to ask you.

   4. Bob needs some help. He has some problems. He needs some advice.

   5. I need to buy some clothes.

   6. I have some homework to do tonight.

   7. I usually get some mail every day.

   8. I usually get some letters every day.

   9. When I'm hungry in the evening, I usually eat some cheese.

   10. We usually do some oral exercises in class every day.

□ EXERCISE 25. Let's talk: pairwork.

   Directions: Work with a partner. Take turns asking and answering questions. Use the words from your list. Remember, you can look at your book before you speak. When you speak, look at your partner.
   Partner A: How **much/many** . . . would you like?
   Partner B: I'd like **a little/a few**, please. Thanks.

   Example: chicken
   PARTNER A: How **much chicken** would you like?
   PARTNER B: I'd like **a little**, please. Thanks.
   PARTNER A: Your turn now.

   Example: pencil
   PARTNER B: How **many pencils** would you like?
   PARTNER A: I'd like **a few**, please.
   PARTNER B: Your turn now.

Partner A	Partner B
1. pen	1. salt
2. tea	2. banana
3. rice	3. soup
4. apple	4. coffee
5. money	5. assignment
6. help	6. cheese
7. toy	7. book

☐ **EXERCISE 26. Sentence review.**

Directions: Complete the sentences with these words. If necessary, use the plural form.

bush	glass	✓ match	strawberry
centimeter	homework	page	thief
dish	inch	paper	tray
edge	information	piece	valley
fish	knife	sex	weather
foot	leaf	size	woman

1. I want to light a candle. I need some ____*matches*____.

2. _____ fall from the trees in autumn.

3. There are two _____: male and female.

4. There are some _____, forks, and spoons on the table.

5. I want to take the bus downtown, but I don't know the bus schedule. I need some

_____ about the bus schedule.

6. I want to write a letter. I have a pen, but I need some _____.

7. Plates and bowls are called _____.

8. Married _____ are called wives.

9. There are a lot of trees and _____ in the park.

10. Bob is studying. He has a lot of _____ to do.

11. My dictionary has 437 _____.

12. This puzzle has 200 _____.

13. A piece of paper has four _____.

14. Mountains are high, and _____
are low.

15. When the temperature is around 35°C (77°F), I'm comfortable. But I don't like

very hot _____.

16. _____ steal things: money, jewelry, cars, etc.

17. _____ are small, red, sweet, and delicious.

18. People carry their food on _____ at a cafeteria.

19. Sweaters in a store often have four _____: small, medium, large, and extra large.

20. In some countries, people use cups for their tea. In other countries, they usually use _____ for their tea.

21. Toshiro has five _____ in his aquarium.

22. There are 100 _____ in a meter.

23. There are 12 _____ in a foot.*

24. There are 3 _____ in a yard.*

7-6 USING *THE*

(a) A: Where's David? B: He's in ***the*** *kitchen.*	A speaker uses ***the*** when the speaker and the listener have the same thing or person in mind. ***The*** shows that a noun is specific.
(b) A: I have two pieces of fruit for us, an apple and a banana. Which do you want? B: I'd like ***the*** *apple,* thank you.	In (a): Both A and B have the same kitchen in mind. In (b): When B says "the apple," both A and B have the same apple in mind.
(c) A: It's a nice summer day today. ***The*** *sky* is blue. ***The*** *sun* is hot. B: Yes, I really like summer.	In (c): Both A and B are thinking of the same sky (there is only one sky for them to think of) and the same sun (there is only one sun for them to think of).
(d) Mike has ***a*** *pen* and ***a*** *pencil.* ***The*** *pen* is blue. ***The*** *pencil* is yellow.	***The*** is used with • singular count nouns, as in (d). • plural count nouns, as in (e). • noncount nouns, as in (f). In other words, ***the*** is used with each of the three kinds of nouns.
(e) Mike has ***some*** *pens and pencils.* ***The*** *pens* are blue. ***The*** *pencils* are yellow.	

(f) Mike has ***some*** *rice* and ***some*** *cheese.*
The *rice* is white.
The *cheese* is yellow.
	Notice in the examples: the speaker is using ***the*** for the **second** mention of a noun. When the speaker mentions a noun for a second time, both the speaker and listener are now thinking about the same thing.
	    First mention: I have ***a*** *pen.*
	    Second mention: ***The*** *pen* is blue.

_____

*1 inch = 2.54 centimeters. 1 foot = 30.48 centimeters. 1 yard = 0.91 meters.

□ EXERCISE 27. Sentence practice.

Directions: Complete the sentences with *the* or *a/an*.

1. I have _____a_____ notebook and _____ grammar book. _____

   notebook is brown. _____ grammar book is red.

2. Right now Pablo is sitting in class. He's sitting between _____ woman and

   _____ man. _____ woman is Graciela. _____ man is Mustafa.

3. Susan is wearing _____ ring and _____ necklace. _____ ring is

   on her left hand.

4. Tony and Sara are waiting for their plane to depart. Tony is reading _____

   magazine. Sara is reading _____ newspaper. When Sara finishes

   _____ newspaper and Tony finishes _____ magazine, they will trade.

5. In the picture below, there are four figures: _____ circle, _____

   triangle, _____ square, and _____ rectangle. _____ circle is

   next to _____ triangle. _____ square is between _____ triangle

   and _____ rectangle.

circle   triangle   square   rectangle

6. Linda and Anne live in _____ apartment in _____ old building. They

   like _____ apartment because it is big. _____ building is very old. It

   was built more than one hundred years ago.

7. I gave my friend _____ card and _____ flower for her birthday.

   _____ card wished her "Happy Birthday." She liked both _____ card

   and _____ flower.

8. We stayed at _____ hotel in New York. _____ hotel was expensive.

☐ **EXERCISE 28. Let's talk: pairwork.**

Directions: Work with a partner. Read the sentences aloud and complete them with **the** or **a/an**. Then change roles. When you have finished speaking, write the answers.

A: Look at the picture below. What do you see?

B: I see _____ chair, _____ desk, _____ window, _____
            1   2   3   4

plant.

A: Where is _____ chair?
                       5

B: _____ chair is under _____ window.
           6   7

A: Where is _____ plant?
                       8

B: _____ plant is beside _____ chair.
           9   10

A: Do you see any people?

B: Yes. I see _____ man and _____ woman. _____ man is
                       11   12   13

standing. _____ woman is sitting down.
                  14

A: Do you see any animals?

B: Yes. I see _____ dog, _____ cat, and _____ bird in
                       15   16   17

_____ cage.
       18

A: What is _____ dog doing?
                     19

B: It's sleeping.

A: How about _____ cat?
                        20

B: _____ cat is watching
           21

_____ bird.
       22

☐ **EXERCISE 29. Review.**

   Directions: Complete the sentences with **the** or **a/an**.

1. A: I need to go shopping. I need to buy _____ coat.

   B: I'll go with you. I need to get _____ umbrella.

   A: Okay. Great! When should we go?

2. A: Hi! Come in!

   B: Hi! _____ weather is terrible today! It's cold and wet outside.

   A: Well, it's warm in here.

   B: What should I do with my coat and umbrella?

   A: You can put _____ coat in that closet. I'll take _____ umbrella

      and put it in _____ kitchen where it can dry.

3. My cousin Jane has _____ good job. She works in _____ office. She

   uses _____ computer.

4. A: How much longer do you need to use _____ computer?

   B: Why?

   A: I need to use it too.

   B: Just five more minutes, then you can have it.

5. A: I need _____ stamp for this letter. Do you have one?

   B: Yes. Here.

   A: Thanks.

6. A: Would you like _____ egg for breakfast?

   B: No thanks. I'll just have _____ glass of juice

      and some toast.

some toast

a toaster

7. A: Do you see my pen? I can't find it.

   B: There it is. It's on _____ floor.

   A: Oh. I see it. Thanks.

8. A: Be sure to look at _____ moon tonight.

   B: Why?

   A: _____ moon is full now, and it's beautiful.

9. A: Can I call you tonight?

   B: No. I don't have _____ telephone in my apartment yet. I just moved in

   yesterday.

10. A: Could you answer _____ telephone? Thanks.

    B: Hello?

7-7 USING Ø (NO ARTICLE) TO MAKE GENERALIZATIONS

(a) **Ø** *Apples* are good for you. (b) **Ø** *Students* use **Ø** *pens* and **Ø** *pencils*. (c) I like to listen to **Ø** *music*. (d) **Ø** *Rice* is good for you.	No article (symbolized by Ø) is used to make generalizations with • plural count nouns, as in (a) and (b), and • noncount nouns, as in (c) and (d).
(e) Tom and Ann ate some fruit. ***The** apples* were very good, but ***the** bananas* were too ripe. (f) We went to a concert last night. ***The** music* was very good.	COMPARE: In (a), the word *apples* is general. It refers to all apples, any apples. No article (Ø) is used. In (e), the word *apples* is specific, so *the* is used in front of it. It refers to the specific apples that Tom and Ann ate. COMPARE: In (c), *music* is general. In (f), *the music* is specific.

□ EXERCISE 30. Sentence practice.
   Directions: Complete the sentences with ***the*** or **Ø** (no article).

   1. ____Ø____ sugar is sweet.

   2. Could you please pass me ____*the*____ sugar?

   3. Oranges are orange, and _____ bananas are yellow.

4. There was some fruit on the table. I didn't eat _____ bananas because they were soft and brown.

5. Everybody needs _____ food to live.

6. We ate at a good restaurant last night. _____ food was excellent.

7. _____ salt tastes salty, and _____ pepper tastes hot.

8. Could you please pass me _____ salt? Thanks. And could I have _____ pepper too?

9. _____ coffee is brown.

10. Steven made some coffee and some tea. _____ coffee was very good.

    I didn't taste _____ tea.

11. _____ pages in this book are full of grammar exercises.

12. _____ books consist of _____ pages.

13. There was some food on the table. The children ate _____ fruit, but they didn't want _____ vegetables.

14. I like _____ fruit. I also like _____ vegetables.

lettuce
a tomato   broccoli
celery

☐ EXERCISE 31. Listening.

👀 *Directions:* Listen to each sentence. Decide if the given noun has a general or a specific use.

1. vegetables   (general)   specific
2. cats   general   specific
3. teacher   general   specific
4. bananas   general   specific
5. cars   general   specific
6. keys   general   specific
7. computers   general   specific
8. ducks   general   specific

☐ EXERCISE 32. Listening: article review.

Directions: Listen to the sentences and write the words you hear. Use *a, an,* or *the.*

1. A: Do you have _____ pen?

   B: There's one on _____ counter in _____ kitchen.

2. A: Where are _____ keys to _____ car?

   B: I'm not sure, but I have _____ set. You can use mine.

3. A: Shh. I hear _____ noise.

   B: It's just _____ bird outside, probably _____

   woodpecker. Don't worry.

4. A: John Jones teaches at _____ university.

   B: I know. He's _____ English professor.

   A: He's also the head of _____ department.

5. A: Hurry! We're late.

   B: No, we're not. It's five o'clock, and we have _____ hour.

   A: No, it isn't. It's six! Look at _____ clock.

   B: Oh my. I need _____ new battery in my watch.

7-8 USING *SOME* AND *ANY*

STATEMENT	(a) Alice has ***some money***.	Use *some* in affirmative statements.
NEGATIVE	(b) Alice doesn't have ***any money***.	Use *any* in negative statements.
QUESTION	(c) Does Alice have ***any money?*** (d) Does Alice have ***some money?***	Use either *some* or *any* in a question.
(e) I don't have ***any money***. (noncount noun) (f) I don't have ***any matches***. (plural count noun)		*Any* is used with noncount nouns and plural count nouns.

☐ EXERCISE 33. Sentence practice.

Directions: Use **some** or **any** to complete the sentences.

1. Sue has _____ some _____ money.

2. I don't have _____ any _____ money.

3. Do you have __ some/any __ money?

4. Do you need _____ help?

5. No, thank you. I don't need _____ help.

6. Ken needs _____ help.

7. Anita usually doesn't get _____ mail.

8. We don't have _____ fruit in the apartment. We don't have

   _____ apples, _____ bananas, or _____ oranges.

9. The house is empty. There aren't _____ people in the house.

10. I need _____ paper. Do you have _____ paper?

11. Heidi can't write a letter because she doesn't have _____ paper.

12. Steve is getting along fine. He doesn't have _____ problems.

13. I need to go to the grocery store. I need to buy _____ food. Do you

    need to buy _____ groceries?

14. I'm not busy tonight. I don't have _____ homework to do.

15. I don't have _____ money in my purse.

16. There are _____ beautiful flowers in my garden this year.

☐ EXERCISE 34. Let's talk: class activity.

Directions: Ask a classmate a question about what he or she sees in this room. Use **any** in the question.

Examples: desks, monkeys
SPEAKER A: *(Speaker B)*, do you see any desks in this room?
SPEAKER B: Yes, I do. I see some desks / a lot of desks / twenty desks.
SPEAKER B: *(Speaker C)*, do you see any monkeys in this room?
SPEAKER C: No, I don't. I don't see any monkeys.
Etc.

1. books	8. paper	15. pillows
2. flowers	9. backpacks	16. red sweaters
3. dictionaries	10. children	17. dogs or cats
4. birds	11. hats	18. bookshelves
5. furniture	12. signs on the wall	19. women
6. food	13. bicycles	20. light bulbs
7. curtains	14. erasers	

☐ EXERCISE 35. Sentence practice.

Directions: Use **any** or **a**. Use **any** with noncount nouns and plural count nouns. Use **a** with singular count nouns.

1. I don't have ___any___ money.

2. I don't have ____a____ pen.

3. I don't have ___any___ brothers or sisters.

4. We don't need to buy _____ new furniture.

5. Mr. and Mrs. Kelly don't have _____ children.

6. I can't make _____ coffee. There isn't _____ coffee in the house.

7. Ann doesn't want _____ cup of coffee.

8. I don't like this room because there aren't _____ windows.

9. Amanda is very unhappy because she doesn't have _____ friends.

10. I don't need _____ help. I can finish my homework by myself.

11. I don't have _____ comfortable chair in my dormitory room.

12. I'm getting along fine. I don't have _____ problems.

13. Joe doesn't have _____ car, so he has to take the bus to school.

14. I don't have _____ homework to do tonight.

15. I don't need _____ new clothes.*

16. I don't need _____ new suit.

_____

Clothes is always plural. The word *clothes* does not have a singular form.

☐ **EXERCISE 36. Chapter review: error analysis.**

Directions: Correct the errors.

                some

1. I need ~~an~~ advice from you.

2. I don't like hot weathers.

3. I usually have a egg for breakfast.

4. Sun rises every morning.

5. The students in this class do a lot of homeworks every day.

6. How many language do you know?

7. I don't have many money.

8. John and Susan don't have some children.

9. A pictures are beautiful. You're a good photographer.

10. There isn't a traffic early in the morning.

11. I can't find any bowl for my soup.

☐ **EXERCISE 37. Review: pairwork.**

Directions: Work in pairs. Ask and answer questions about the things and people in the picture on p. 209.

Example:
PARTNER A: How many boys are there in the picture?
PARTNER B: There are three boys in the picture.
PARTNER A: Are there any flowers?
PARTNER B: No, there aren't any flowers in the picture.
PARTNER A: Are you sure?
PARTNER B: Well, hmmm. I don't see any flowers.
PARTNER A: Oh?
Etc.

☐ EXERCISE 38. Sentence practice.

   Directions: Make the nouns plural where necessary.

                              cities
   1. Toronto and Bangkok are big ~~city.~~

   2. I need some information. *(no change)*

   3. Horse are large animals.

   4. I like to listen to music when I study.

   5. I have two small child.

   6. I like to tell them story.

   7. There are sixty minute in an hour.

   8. Children like to play with toy.

   9. My bookcase has three shelf.

   10. There are five woman and seven man in this class.

   11. Taiwan and Cuba are island.

   12. I drink eight glass of water every day.

   13. Tomato are red when they are ripe.

   14. Before dinner, I put dish, spoon, fork, knife, and napkin on the table.

   15. I have many friend. I don't have many enemy.

☐ EXERCISE 39. Let's talk: review.

   Directions: Imagine that a new shopping center is coming to your neighborhood. A drugstore and a grocery store are already in place. Decide what other stores you want to add. Your teacher will help you with vocabulary you don't know.

   PART I. Work alone.

   Choose any six businesses from the list and write their names in any of the six available spaces on Blueprint #1 on p. 211.

✓ a bank	✓ a grocery store	a post office
a bookstore	an ice-cream shop	a shoe store
a camera shop	an Internet café	a sports equipment store
✓ a drugstore	a laundromat	a vegetarian food store
a drycleaner's	a movie theater	a video rental store
an exercise gym	a music store	
a fast-food restaurant	a pet supply store	

BLUEPRINT #1
(your business locations)

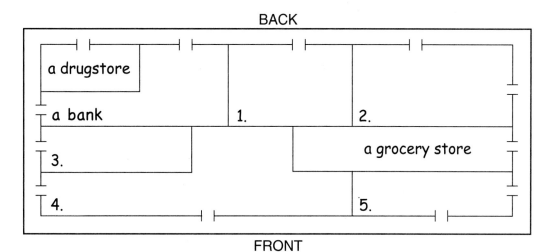

PART II. Work with a partner, but do not look at each other's blueprints.

Partner A: Ask your partner about the location of his/her new businesses.
Write your partner's answers on your copy of Blueprint #2.

Partner B: Ask your partner about the location of his/her new businesses.
Write your partner's answers on your copy of Blueprint #2.

When you are finished, compare your answers. Does your Blueprint #1 match your partner's Blueprint #2?

Question and answer pattern.

PARTNER A: Is there **a/an** _____?

PARTNER B: Yes, there is. / No, there isn't.

PARTNER A: Where is **the** _____?

PARTNER B: It's next to / beside / in back of / in front of **the** _____.

Example:

PARTNER A: Is there **an** exercise gym?

PARTNER B: No, there isn't.

PARTNER A: Is there **a** bank?

PARTNER B: Yes, there is.

PARTNER A: Where is **the** bank?

PARTNER B: It's in front of **the** drugstore.

BLUEPRINT #2
(your partner's business locations)

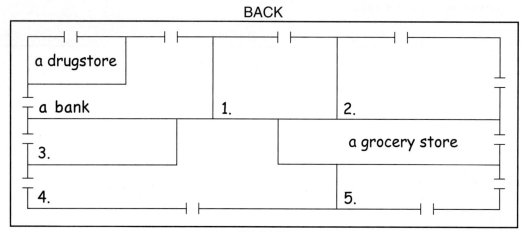

CHAPTER 8
Expressing Past Time, Part 1

8-1 USING *BE:* PAST TIME

PRESENT TIME	PAST TIME
(a) I *am* in class *today*.	(b) I *was* in class *yesterday*.
(c) Alice *is* at the library *today*.	(d) Alice *was* at the library *yesterday*.
(e) My friends *are* at home *today*.	(f) My friends *were* at home *yesterday*.

SIMPLE PAST TENSE OF *BE*

Singular	Plural
I was	*we were*
you were (one person)	*you were* (more than one person)
she was	*they were*
he was	
it was	

$$\left.\begin{matrix} I \\ she \\ he \\ it \end{matrix}\right\} \; + \; was$$

$$\left.\begin{matrix} we \\ you \\ they \end{matrix}\right\} \; + \; were$$

☐ EXERCISE 1. Sentence practice.

Directions: Change the sentences to past time.

1. Bob is in class today. → *He was in class yesterday too.*

2. I'm in class today. → *I was in class yesterday too.*

3. Mary is at the library today.

4. We're in class today.

5. You're busy today.

6. I'm happy today.

7. The classroom is hot today.

8. Ann is in her office today.

9. Tom is in his office today.

10. Ann and Tom are in their offices today.

☐ EXERCISE 2. Let's talk: class activity.

Directions: Talk about today and yesterday. Close your book for this activity.

Example:

TEACHER: I'm in class.
SPEAKER A: I'm in class **today**. I was in class **yesterday too**.
TEACHER: *(to Speaker B) (Speaker A)* is in class.
SPEAKER B: *(Speaker A)* is in class **today**. She/He was in class **yesterday too**.

1. We're in class.
2. I'm in class.
3. (. . .) is in class.
4. (. . .) and (. . .) are in class.
5. (. . .) is here.
6. (. . .) is absent.
7. I'm tired.
8. (. . .) and (. . .) are *(in the first row)*.
9. The door is open/closed.
10. It's hot/cold.

8-2 PAST OF *BE:* NEGATIVE

(a) I *was not* in class yesterday. (b) I *wasn't* in class yesterday.	NEGATIVE CONTRACTIONS *was* + *not* = *wasn't* *were* + *not* = *weren't*
(c) They *were not* at home last night. (d) They *weren't* at home last night.	I she he it } + *wasn't* we you they } + *weren't*

☐ EXERCISE 3. Sentence practice.

Directions: Study the time expressions. Then complete the sentences. Use *wasn't* or *weren't*. Use a past time expression.

PRESENT		PAST
today	→	*yesterday*
this morning	→	*yesterday morning*
this afternoon	→	*yesterday afternoon*
tonight	→	*last night*
this week	→	*last week*

1. Ken is here today, but _____ *he wasn't here yesterday.* _____

2. I'm at home tonight, but _____ *I wasn't at home last night.* _____

3. Olga is busy today, but _____

4. Tom is at the library tonight, but _____

5. Alex and Rita are at work this afternoon, but _____

6. You're here today, but _____

7. Dr. Ruckman is in her office this morning, but _____

8. It's cold this week, but _____

□ EXERCISE 4. Let's talk: class activity.
Directions: Think about your first day in this class. Check (✓) the words that describe how you felt. Then answer your teacher's questions.

Example: happy
TEACHER: Were you happy the first day of class?
SPEAKER A: Yes, I was happy.
SPEAKER B: No, I wasn't happy.
TEACHER: (to Speaker C) Tell me about (Speaker A) and (Speaker B).
SPEAKER C: (Speaker A) was happy. (Speaker B) wasn't happy.

1. _____ excited   4. _____ relaxed (not nervous)

2. _____ scared/afraid   5. _____ quiet

3. _____ nervous   6. _____ talkative

□ EXERCISE 5. Listening.
Directions: Listen to the sentences. Circle the verbs you hear.

1. was	(wasn't)		6. were	weren't
2. was	wasn't		7. was	wasn't
3. was	wasn't		8. was	wasn't
4. was	wasn't		9. were	weren't
5. were	weren't		10. were	weren't

□ EXERCISE 6. Let's talk: find someone who . . . .
Directions: Interview your classmates about their days in elementary school. Find people who can answer yes to your questions. Write down their names.
Speaker A: Make a complete question with the given words. Use the past tense.
          Ask (Speaker B) the question.
Speaker B: Answer the question.

Example: you \ shy

SPEAKER A: Were you shy?
SPEAKER B: No, I wasn't.
SPEAKER A: *(to Speaker C)* Were you shy?
SPEAKER C: Yes, I was.

	First name
1. you \ shy	
2. you \ outgoing (not shy)	
3. you \ talkative	
4. you \ happy	
5. you \ hardworking	
6. you \ quiet	

	First name
7. you \ noisy	
8. you \ athletic	
9. you \ active	
10. you \ well-behaved	
11. you \ a serious student	
12. you \ artistic	

8-3 PAST OF *BE:* QUESTIONS

YES/NO QUESTIONS		SHORT ANSWER + (LONG ANSWER)	
(a) **Were** **you** in class yesterday? *(be)* + (subject)	→ →	**Yes, I was.** **No, I wasn't.**	(I was in class yesterday.) (I wasn't in class yesterday.)
(b) **Was** **Carlos** at home last night? *(be)* + (subject)	→	**Yes, he was.** **No, he wasn't.**	(He was at home last night.) (He wasn't at home last night.)
INFORMATION QUESTIONS		SHORT ANSWER + (LONG ANSWER)	
(c) **Where** **were** **you** yesterday? Where + *(be)* + (subject)	→	**In class.**	(I was in class yesterday.)
(d) **Where** **was** **Jennifer** last night? Where + *(be)* + (subject)	→	**At home.**	(She was at home last night.)

☐ EXERCISE 7. Question practice.

   Directions: Make questions and give short answers.

1. *(you \ at home \ last night)*

   A: _____*Were you at home last night?*_____

   B: No, _____*I wasn't.*_____

2. *(Mr. Yamamoto \ absent from class \ yesterday)*

   A: _____

   B: Yes, _____

3. *(Oscar and Anya \ at home \ last night)*

   A: _____

   B: Yes, _____

4. *(you \ nervous \ the first day of class)*

   A: _____

   B: No, _____

5. *(Ahmed \ at the library \ last night)*

   A: _____

   B: Yes, _____

6. *(Mr. Shin \ in class \ yesterday)*

   A: _____

   B: No, _____

   A: Where _____

   B: At home.

7. *(you and your family \ in Canada \ last year)*

A: _____

B: No, _____

A: Where _____

B: In Ireland.

8. *(you \ be \ at the library \ right now)*

A: _____

B: No, _____

A: Where _____

B: In class.

☐ EXERCISE 8. Let's talk: pairwork.

Directions: Work with a partner. Ask and answer questions. If your partner answers *yes,* the exercise item is finished. If your partner answers *no,* ask a *where*-question.

Example: in class \ now
PARTNER A *(book open):* (Partner B), are you in class now?
PARTNER B *(book closed):* Yes, I am.

Example: at the library \ last night
PARTNER A *(book open):* (Partner B), were you at the library last night?
PARTNER B *(book closed):* No, I wasn't.
PARTNER A *(book open):* Where were you?
PARTNER B *(book closed):* I was (at home \ in my room \ at a party, etc.).

1. at home \ now
2. at home \ yesterday morning
3. at home \ last night
4. in class \ six hours ago
5. in *(a place in this city)* \ now
6. in *(this city)* \ last year
7. *(your teacher)* \ in class \ yesterday
8. *(two classmates)* \ here \ yesterday

Switch roles.
Partner A: Close your book.
Partner B: Open your book. Your turn now.

9. in *(this country)* \ two weeks ago
10. in *(this country)* \ two years ago
11. in *(a city)* \ now
12. at *(a park in this city)* \ yesterday afternoon

13. at *(a famous place in this city)* \ this morning*
14. at *(a popular place for students)* \ last night
15. at home \ this morning
16. *(two students)* \ *(this building)* \ yesterday afternoon

☐ EXERCISE 9. Question practice.
   Directions: Make questions and give short answers.

   1. *(you \ in class \ yesterday)*

      A: _____*Were you in class yesterday?*_____

      B: Yes, _____*I was.*_____

   2. *(Anita \ in class \ today)*

      A: _____*Is Anita in class today?*_____

      B: No, _____*she isn't.*_____ She's absent.

   3. *(you \ tired \ last night)*

      A: _____

      B: Yes, _____. I went to bed early.

   4. *(you \ hungry \ right now)*

      A: _____

      B: No, _____, but I'm thirsty.

   5. *(the weather \ hot in New York City \ last summer)*

      A: _____

      B: Yes, _____. It was very hot.

   6. *(the weather \ cold in Alaska \ in the winter)*

      A: _____

      B: Yes, _____. It's very cold.

------

*If you are asking this question in the morning, use a present verb. If it is now afternoon or evening, use a past verb.

7. (*Yoko and Mohammed \ here \ yesterday afternoon*)

A: _____

B: Yes, _____

8. *(the students \ in this class \ intelligent)*

A: _____

B: Of course _____! They are very intelligent!

9. *(Mr. Tok \ absent \ today)*

A: _____

B: Yes, _____

A: Where _____

B: _____

10. (*Tony and Benito \ at the party \ last night*)

A: _____

B: No, _____

A: Where _____

B: _____

11. *(Amy \ out of town \ last week)*

A: _____

B: Yes, _____

A: Where _____

B: _____

_____

12. *(Mr. and Mrs. Rice \ in town \ this week)*

A: _____

B: No, _____. They're out of town.

A: Oh? Where _____

B: _____

8-4 THE SIMPLE PAST TENSE: USING -ED

SIMPLE PRESENT SIMPLE PAST	(a) I **walk** to school **every day**. (b) I **walked** to school **yesterday**.	verb + **-ed** = the simple past tense *I*
SIMPLE PRESENT SIMPLE PAST	(c) Ann **walks** to school **every day**. (d) Ann **walked** to school **yesterday**.	*you* *she* *he* } + *walked (verb + **-ed**)* *it* *we* *they*

☐ EXERCISE 10. Sentence practice.
    Directions: Complete the sentences orally in the simple past. Then write the answers.

1. Every day I walk. Yesterday I _____ .

2. Every day I work. Yesterday I _____ .

3. Every day Omar shaves. Yesterday Omar _____ .

4. Every night Paula watches TV. Last night she _____ TV.

5. Every day Mrs. Wu cooks. Last night she _____ .

6. Every day people smile. Yesterday they _____ .

7. Every week it rains. Last week it _____ .

8. Every day we ask questions. Yesterday we _____ questions.

9. Every day I talk on the phone. Yesterday I _____ on the phone.

10. Every day Tomo listens to music. Yesterday he _____ to music.

□ EXERCISE 11. Sentence practice.

Directions: Complete the sentences. Use the words in the list. Use the simple present or the simple past.

ask	erase	smile	walk
cook	✓rain	stay	watch
dream	shave	wait	work

1. It often _____*rains*_____ in the morning. It _____*rained*_____ yesterday.

2. I _____ to school every morning. I _____ to school yesterday morning.

3. Sue often _____ questions. She _____ a question in class yesterday.

4. I _____ a movie on television last night. I usually

   _____ TV in the evening because I want to improve my English.

5. Mike _____ his own dinner yesterday evening. He

   _____ his own dinner every evening.

6. I usually _____ home at night because I have to study. I

   _____ home last night.

7. I have a job at the library. I _____ at the library every evening.

   I _____ there yesterday evening.

8. When I am asleep, I often _____. I _____ about my family last night.*

9. Linda usually _____ for the bus at a bus stop in front of her

   apartment building. She _____ for the bus there yesterday

   morning.

10. The teacher _____ some words from the board a couple of

    minutes ago. He used his hand instead of an eraser.

————————

*The past of *dream* can be *dreamed* or *dreamt*.

11. Our teacher is a warm, friendly person. She often _____ when she is talking to us.

12. Rick doesn't have a beard anymore. He _____ it five days ago.

Now he _____ every morning.

☐ **EXERCISE 12. Let's talk: pairwork.**

Directions: Work with a partner. Check (✓) all the activities you did yesterday. Tell your partner. Begin with ***Yesterday I*** . . . . Share a few of your partner's answers with the class.

1. _____ ask the teacher a question
2. _____ cook dinner
3. _____ wash some clothes
4. _____ listen to music on the radio
5. _____ use a computer
6. _____ stay home in the evening
7. _____ walk in a park

8. _____ watch TV
9. _____ work at my desk
10. _____ wait for a bus
11. _____ smile at several people
12. _____ talk on a cell phone
13. _____ dream in English
14. _____ dream in my language

☐ **EXERCISE 13. Pronunciation practice.**

Directions: Pronounce the words in each group.

GROUP A: Final **-ed** is pronounced /t/ if the verb ends in a voiceless sound.*
1. walked   3. laughed   5. missed   7. stretched
2. washed   4. helped   6. sniffed   8. watched

GROUP B: Final **-ed** is pronounced /d/ if the verb ends in a voiced sound.
1. closed   3. rubbed   5. filled   7. loved   9. stirred
2. waited   4. turned   6. seemed   8. stayed   10. hugged

GROUP C: Final **-ed** is pronounced /əd/ if the verb ends in the letter "d" or "t."
1. rent   2. need   3. visit   4. add

_____

*See Chart 3-8, p. 66, for information about voiceless and voiced sounds.

Directions: Listen to each sentence and circle the verb you hear.

1. play   plays   (played)

2. play   plays   played

3. watch   watches   watched

4. enjoy   enjoys   enjoyed

5. watch   watches   watched

6. ask   asks   asked

7. answer   answers   answered

8. listen   listens   listened

9. like   likes   liked

10. work   works   worked

☐ EXERCISE 15. Let's talk: class activity.

Directions: Answer the questions your teacher asks you. Practice pronouncing **-ed**. Close your book for this activity.

Example: walk to the front of the room
TEACHER: *(Speaker A),* walk to the front of the room.
SPEAKER A: *(walks to the front of the room)*
TEACHER: *(to Speaker B)* What did *(Speaker A)* do?
SPEAKER B: She/He walked to the front of the room.
TEACHER: *(to Speaker A)* What did you do?
SPEAKER A: I walked to the front of the room.

1. smile
2. laugh
3. cough
4. sneeze
5. shave *(pantomime)*
6. erase the board
7. sign your name
8. open the door
9. close the door
10. ask a question
11. wash your hands *(pantomime)*
12. touch the floor
13. point at the door
14. fold a piece of paper
15. count your fingers
16. push *(something in the room)*
17. pull *(something in the room)*
18. yawn
19. pick up your pen
20. add two and two on the board

8-5 PAST TIME WORDS: *YESTERDAY, LAST,* AND *AGO*

YESTERDAY	*LAST*	*AGO*

(a) Bob was here . . .
    yesterday.
    yesterday morning.
    yesterday afternoon.
    yesterday evening.
	(b) Sue was here . . .
	    last night.
	    last week.
	    last month.
	    last year.
	
	    last spring.
	    last summer.
	    last fall.
	    last winter.
	
	    last Monday.
	    last Tuesday.
	    last Wednesday.
	    etc.
		(c) Tom was here . . .
		    five minutes ago.
		    two hours ago.
		    three days ago.
		    a (one) week ago.
		    six months ago.
		    a (one) year ago.

NOTICE

In (a): *yesterday* is used with *morning, afternoon,* and *evening.*

In (b): *last* is used with *night,* with long periods of time *(week, month, year),* with seasons *(spring, summer, etc.),* and with days of the week.

In (c): *ago* means "in the past." It follows specific lengths of time (e.g., *two minutes* + *ago, five years* + *ago).*

☐ EXERCISE 16. Sentence practice.

Directions: Complete the sentences. Use *yesterday* or *last.*

1. I dreamed about you _____*last*_____ night.

2. I was downtown _____ morning.

3. Two students were absent _____ Friday.

4. Ann wasn't at home _____ night.

5. Ann wasn't at home _____ evening.

6. Carmen was out of town _____ week.

7. I visited my aunt and uncle _____ fall.

8. Roberto walked home _____ afternoon.

9. My sister arrived in Miami _____ Sunday.

10. We watched TV _____ night.

11. Ali played with his children _____ evening.

12. Yoko arrived in Los Angeles _____ summer.

13. I visited my relatives in San Francisco _____ month.

14. My wife and I moved into a new house _____ year.

15. Mrs. Porter washed the kitchen floor _____ morning.

☐ EXERCISE 17. Sentence practice.

> *Directions:* Complete the sentences with your own words. Use **ago**.

1. I'm in class now, but I was at home _____ *ten minutes ago / two hours ago / etc.*

2. I'm in class today, but I was absent from class _____

3. I'm in this country now, but I was in my country _____

4. I was in *(name of a city)* _____

5. I was in elementary school _____

6. I arrived in this city _____

7. There is a nice park in this city. I was at the park _____

8. We finished Exercise 16 _____

9. I was home in bed _____

10. It rained in this city _____

☐ EXERCISE 18. Listening.

> *Directions:* Listen to the sentences and answer the questions.

PART I. Write today's date.

Today's date is _____.

Listen to the sentences and write the dates.

1. _____.   5. _____.

2. _____.   6. _____.

3. _____.   7. _____.

4. _____.

PART II. Write the correct time.

Right now, the time is _____.

Listen to the sentences and write the times you hear.

8. _____.

9. _____.

10. _____.

8-6 THE SIMPLE PAST: IRREGULAR VERBS (GROUP 1)

Some verbs do not have *-ed* forms. Their past forms are irregular.

PRESENT PAST	
come – came *do – did* *eat – ate* *get – got* *go – went* *have – had* *put – put* *see – saw* *sit – sat* *sleep – slept* *stand – stood* *write – wrote*	(a) I *come* to class *every day.* (b) I *came* to class *yesterday.* (c) I *do* my homework *every day.* (d) I *did* my homework *yesterday.* (e) Ann *eats* breakfast *every morning.* (f) Ann *ate* breakfast *yesterday morning.*

☐ **EXERCISE 19. Let's talk: class activity.**

Directions: Practice using irregular verbs. Close your book for this activity.

Example: ***come–came***

TEACHER: come–came. I come to class every day. I came to class yesterday.
          What did I do yesterday?
STUDENTS: *(repeat)* come–came. You came to class yesterday.

1. ***do–did***   We do exercises in class every day. We did exercises yesterday. What did we do yesterday?

2. ***eat–ate***   I eat lunch at 12:00 every day. Yesterday I ate lunch at 12:00. What did I do at 12:00 yesterday?

3. ***get–got***   I get up early every day. I got up early yesterday. What did I do yesterday? Did you get up early yesterday? What time did you get up?

4. **go–went**   I go downtown every day. I went downtown yesterday. What did I do yesterday? Did you go downtown? Where did you go?

5. **have–had**   I have breakfast every morning. I had breakfast yesterday morning. What did I do yesterday morning? I had toast and fruit for breakfast. What did you have?

6. **put–put**   I like hats. I put on a hat every day. What did I do yesterday?

7. **see–saw**   I see my best friend every day. Yesterday I saw my best friend. What did I do yesterday? Did you see your best friend? Who did you see?

8. **sit–sat**   I usually sit at my desk in the mornings. I sat at my desk yesterday morning. What did I do yesterday morning?

9. **sleep–slept**   Sometimes I sleep for a long time at night. I slept for 10 hours last night. What did I do last night? Did you sleep for 10 hours last night? How long did you sleep last night?

10. **stand–stood**   I stand at the bus stop every day. I stood at the bus stop yesterday. What did I do yesterday?

11. **write–wrote**   I usually write in my journal every day. Yesterday I wrote in my journal. What did I do yesterday? Did you write in your journal? What did you write about?

☐ EXERCISE 20. Let's talk: pairwork.

Directions: Work with a partner. Take turns changing the sentences from the present to the past.

Example: I have class every day.
PARTNER A: I have class every day. I had class yesterday. Your turn now.

Example: Roberto gets mail from home every week.
PARTNER B: Roberto gets mail from home every week. Roberto got mail from home last week. Your turn now.

Partner A
1. Rita gets some mail every day.
2. They go downtown every day.
3. The students stand in line at the cafeteria every day.
4. I see my friends every day.
5. Hamid sits in the front row every day.
6. I sleep for eight hours every night.

Partner B
1. We have lunch every day.
2. I write e-mails to my parents every week.
3. Wai-Leng comes to class late every day.
4. I do my homework every day.
5. I eat breakfast every morning.
6. Roberto puts his books in his briefcase every day.

☐ EXERCISE 21. Verb review.

Directions: Complete the sentences. Use the words in parentheses. Use the simple present, the present progressive, or the simple past. Pay attention to spelling.

1. I *(get)* _____got_____ up at eight o'clock yesterday morning.

2. Mary *(talk)* _____ to John on the phone last night.

3. Mary *(talk)* _____ to John on the phone right now.

4. Mary *(talk)* _____ to John on the phone every day.

5. Jim and I *(eat)* _____ lunch at the cafeteria two hours ago.

6. We *(eat)* _____ lunch at the cafeteria every day.

7. I *(go)* _____ to bed early last night.

8. My roommate *(study)* _____ Spanish last year.

9. Sue *(write)* _____ an e-mail to her parents yesterday.

10. Sue *(write)* _____ an e-mail to her parents every week.

11. Sue is in her room right now. She *(sit)* _____ at her desk.

12. Maria *(do)* _____ her homework last night.

13. Yesterday I *(see)* _____ Fumiko at the library.

14. I *(have)* _____ a dream last night. I *(dream)*

_____ about my friends. I *(sleep)* _____

for eight hours.

15. A strange thing *(happen)* _____ to me yesterday. I

couldn't remember my own telephone number.

16. My wife *(come)* _____ home around five every day.

17. Yesterday she *(come)* _____ home at 5:15.

18. Our teacher *(stand)* _____ in the middle of the room

right now.

19. Our teacher *(stand)* _____ in the front of the room

yesterday.

20. Tom *(put)* _____ the butter in the refrigerator yesterday.

21. He *(put)* _____ the milk in the refrigerator every day.

22. Pablo usually *(sit)* _____ in the back of the room, but

yesterday he *(sit)* _____ in the front row. Today he *(be)*

_____ absent. He *(be)* _____

absent two days ago too.

☐ EXERCISE 22. Listening.

Directions: Listen to the beginning of each sentence. Circle the correct completion(s). There may be more than one correct answer.

Example: He did . . . . (his homework) (a good job) absent

1. a chair	some rice	some numbers
2. on the floor	a man	together
3. late	yesterday	car
4. an answer	pretty	a book
5. a good grade	last month	a new truck
6. a watch	next to my parents	at the bus stop

☐ EXERCISE 23. Let's talk: small groups.

Directions: Work in small groups. Use numbers to put the sentences in correct story order. Then finish the story. Share it with the class.

__2__ He looked up at the stars.

_____ He put the postcard down and went to sleep.

_____ The bear stood next to his tent.

_____ The next morning, John sat up and rubbed his eyes.

__1__ One night, John went camping.

_____ They were beautiful.

_____ He wrote a postcard to his girlfriend.

_____ The bear had his postcard.

_____ He saw a bear.

8-7 THE SIMPLE PAST: NEGATIVE

	SUBJECT	+ *DID*	+ *NOT*	+ MAIN VERB	
(a)	I	*did*	*not*	*walk*	to school yesterday.
(b)	You	*did*	*not*	*walk*	to school yesterday.
(c)	Tom	*did*	*not*	*eat*	lunch yesterday.
(d)	They	*did*	*not*	*come*	to class yesterday.

INCORRECT: *I did not walked to school yesterday.*
INCORRECT: *Tom did not ate lunch yesterday.*

I
you
she
he } + *did not* + main verb*
it
we
they

Notice: The simple form of the main verb is used with *did not*.

(e)	I *didn't walk* to school yesterday.
(f)	Tom *didn't eat* lunch yesterday.

NEGATIVE CONTRACTION
did + *not* = *didn't*

*EXCEPTION: *did* is NOT used when the main verb is *be*. See Charts 8-2, p. 214, and 8-3, p. 216.
    CORRECT: Joe *wasn't* here yesterday.
    INCORRECT: Joe *didn't be* here yesterday.

☐ EXERCISE 24. Sentence practice.
    Directions: Complete the sentences. Use *not*.

    1. I don't go to the park every day. I went to the park last week, but I
          ___*didn't go*___ there yesterday.

    2. We don't have rain every day. We had rain two days ago, but we
          _____ rain yesterday.

    3. Linda doesn't sit in the front row every day. She sat there yesterday, but she
          _____ there two days ago.

    4. Mrs. Romano and her son don't talk on the phone every day. They talked to each
          other last weekend, but they _____ on the phone last night.

☐ EXERCISE 25. Let's talk: pairwork.
    Directions: Work with a partner. Take turns using *I don't ... every day* and *I didn't
    ... yesterday*.

    Example: walk to school
    PARTNER A: I don't walk to school every day. I didn't walk to school yesterday. Your
            turn now.

    Example: listen to the radio
    PARTNER B: I don't listen to the radio every day. I didn't listen to the radio yesterday.
            Your turn now.

Partner A	Partner B
1. eat breakfast	1. go to the library
2. watch TV	2. visit my friends
3. go shopping	3. see *(name of a person)*
4. read a newspaper	4. do my homework
5. study	5. get on the Internet

☐ **EXERCISE 26. Let's talk: class activity.**

Directions: Practice present and past negatives. Close your books for this activity.

Speaker A: Use *I don't* and *I didn't*. Use an appropriate past time expression with *didn't*.

Speaker B: Report what Speaker A said. Use *She/He doesn't* and then *She/He didn't* with an appropriate past time expression.

Example: walk to school every morning

TEACHER: walk to school every morning

SPEAKER A: I don't walk to school every morning. I didn't walk to school yesterday morning.

TEACHER: *(to Speaker B)* Tell me about *(Speaker A)*.

SPEAKER B: She/He doesn't walk to school every morning. She/He didn't walk to school yesterday morning.

1. eat breakfast every morning
2. watch TV every night
3. talk to *(someone)* every day
4. play soccer every afternoon
5. study grammar every evening

6. dream in English every night
7. visit my aunt and uncle every year
8. write to my parents every week
9. read the newspaper every morning
10. pay all of my bills every month

☐ **EXERCISE 27. Sentence practice.**

Directions: Complete the sentences. Use the words in parentheses. Use simple present, simple past, or present progressive.

1. Jasmin *(come, not)* _____didn't come_____ to the meeting yesterday. She

   (stay) _____ in her office.

2. I *(go)* _____ to a movie last night, but I *(enjoy, not)*

   _____ it. It *(be, not)* _____ very good.

3. Sue (read) _____ a magazine right now. She (watch, not)

_____ TV. She (like, not) _____ to

watch TV during the day.

4. Toshi is a busy student. Sometimes he (eat, not) _____

lunch because he (have, not) _____ enough time between

classes. Yesterday he (have, not) _____ time for lunch. He

(get) _____ hungry during his afternoon class.

☐ EXERCISE 28. Let's talk: small groups.
   Directions: Work in groups of six to eight students. Tell your group things you ***didn't
   do yesterday***. Repeat the information from the other students in your group.

Example:
SPEAKER A: I didn't go to the zoo yesterday.
SPEAKER B: *(Speaker A)* didn't go to the zoo yesterday. I didn't have lunch in Beijing
           yesterday.
SPEAKER C: *(Speaker A)* didn't go to the zoo yesterday. *(Speaker B)* didn't have lunch
           in Beijing yesterday. I didn't swim in the Pacific Ocean yesterday.
Etc.

Suggestions:

go *(someplace)*	drive to *(a place)*
walk to *(a place)*	fly to *(a place)*
have *(a meal)*	study *(a subject)*
eat *(something)*	buy *(something)*
swim *(in a place)*	sleep in *(a place)*
sing *(in the shower)*	wear *(something)*
visit *(a person)*	see *(someone)*
talk to *(a person)*	wake up *(at a time)*
use *(something)*	

8-8 THE SIMPLE PAST: YES/NO QUESTIONS

DID + SUBJECT + MAIN VERB	SHORT ANSWER + (LONG ANSWER)
(a) **Did** **Mary** **walk** to school? →	**Yes, she did.** (She walked to school.)
	→ **No, she didn't.** (She didn't walk to school.)
(b) **Did** **you** **come** to class? →	**Yes, I did.** (I came to class.)
	→ **No, I didn't.** (I didn't come to class.)

☐ EXERCISE 29. Question practice.

Directions: Make questions. Give short answers.

1. A: _____Did you walk downtown yesterday?_____

   B: _____Yes, I did._____ (I walked downtown yesterday.)

2. A: _____Did it rain last week?_____

   B: _____No, it didn't._____ (It didn't rain last week.)

3. A: _____

   B: _____ (I ate lunch at the cafeteria.)

4. A: _____

   B: _____ (Mr. Kwan didn't go out of town last week.)

5. A: _____

   B: _____ (I had a cup of tea this morning.)

6. A: _____

   B: _____ (Benito and I went to a party last night.)

7. A: _____

   B: _____ (Olga studied English in high school.)

8. A: _____

   B: _____ (Yoko and Ali didn't do their homework last night.)

9. A: _____

   B: _____ (I saw Gina at dinner last night.)

10. A: _____

    B: _____ (I didn't dream in English last night.)

☐ EXERCISE 30. Listening.

Directions: Listen to the questions and write the words you hear.

Example:
You will hear: Did you eat breakfast this morning?
You will write: _____*Did you*_____ eat breakfast this morning?

1. _____ do well on the test?

2. _____ finish the assignment?

3. _____ make sense?

4. _____ answer your question?

5. _____ need more help?

6. _____ understand the homework?

7. _____ explain the project?

8. _____ complete the project?

9. _____ do well?

10. _____ pass the class?

☐ EXERCISE 31. Let's talk: pairwork.

Directions: Work with a partner. Ask questions about her/his activities this morning.

Example: walk to school
PARTNER A *(book open):* Did you walk to school this morning?
PARTNER B *(book closed):* Yes, I did. OR No, I didn't.

1. get up at seven
2. eat breakfast
3. study English
4. walk to class
5. talk to *(name of a person)*
6. see *(name of a person)*

Switch roles.
Partner A: Close your book.
Partner B: Open your book. Your turn to talk now.

7. make your bed
8. go shopping
9. have a cup of tea
10. watch TV
11. listen to the radio
12. read a newspaper

☐ **EXERCISE 32. Let's talk: find someone who . . . .**

Directions: Interview your classmates. Find people who can answer *yes* to your questions. Write down their names.
Speaker A: Make a complete question with the given verb. Use the past tense. Ask *(Speaker B)* the question.
Speaker B: Answer the question. Give both a short answer and a long answer.

Example: eat ice cream \ yesterday?
SPEAKER A: Did you eat ice cream yesterday?
SPEAKER B: No, I didn't.
SPEAKER A: *(Ask another student.)* Did you eat ice cream yesterday?
SPEAKER C: Yes, I did. I ate ice cream yesterday.

	First name
1. eat rice \ yesterday	
2. do homework \ last night	
3. get an e-mail \ yesterday	
4. go shopping \ yesterday	
5. sleep well \ last night	
6. a. have coffee for breakfast \ this morning b. put sugar in your coffee \ this morning	
7. see a good movie \ last week	
8. write in English \ today	
9. sit on the floor \ yesterday	
10. stand in line for something \ last week	

☐ EXERCISE 33. Listening.

Directions: Listen to the reductions in spoken English. In spoken questions, *did* and the pronoun that follows are often reduced.

PART I. Listen to the examples.

1. **Did you** ("dih-juh") read the paper this morning?

2. A: Tom called.

   B: **Did he** ("dih-de") leave a message?

3. A: Sara called.

   B: **Did she** ("dih-she") leave a message?

4. **Did it** ("dih-dit") rain yesterday?

5. A: The children are watching TV.

   B: **Did they** ("dih-they") finish their homework?

6. I can't find my notebook. **Did I** ("dih-di") leave it on your desk?

PART II. Listen to the sentences. You will hear reduced speech *did* + *pronoun*. Write the non-reduced forms.

Examples:
You will hear: "Dih-dit" rain yesterday?
You will write: _____*Did it*_____ rain yesterday?

You will hear: "Dih-juh" come to class yesterday?
You will write: _____*Did you*_____ come to class yesterday?

1. _____ finish the homework assignment?

2. _____ take a long time?

3. _____ hear my question?

4. _____ hear my question?

5. _____ speak loud enough?

6. _____ understand the information?

7. _____ understand the information?

8. _____ want more help?

9. _____ explain it okay?

10. _____ do a good job?

8-9 IRREGULAR VERBS (GROUP 2)

bring – brought	*drive – drove*	*run – ran*
buy – bought	*read – read★*	*teach – taught*
catch – caught	*ride – rode*	*think – thought*
drink – drank		

★The past form of *read* is pronounced the same as the color *red*.

☐ EXERCISE 34. Let's talk: class activity.

Directions: Practice using irregular verbs. Close your book for this activity.

Example: **teach–taught**
TEACHER: teach–taught. I teach class every day. I taught class yesterday. What did I do yesterday?
STUDENTS: *(repeat)* teach–taught. You taught class.

1. **bring–brought**   I bring my book to class every day. I brought my book to class yesterday. What did I do yesterday?

2. **buy–bought**   I buy books at the bookstore. I bought a book yesterday. What did I do yesterday?

3. **catch–caught**   I catch the bus every day. I caught the bus yesterday. What did I do yesterday? Sometimes I catch a cold. Yesterday I caught a bad cold. What did I do yesterday?

4. **think–thought**   I often think about my family. I thought about my family yesterday. What did I do yesterday?

5. **REVIEW:**   What did I bring to class yesterday? What did you bring yesterday? What did I buy yesterday? What did you buy yesterday? Did you teach class yesterday? Who did? Did I walk to class yesterday, or did I catch the bus? What did I think about yesterday? What did you think about yesterday?

6. **run–ran**   Sometimes I'm late for class, so I run. Yesterday I was late, so I ran. What did I do yesterday?

7. **read–read**   I like to read books. I read every day. Yesterday I read a book. What did I do yesterday? What did you read yesterday?

8. **drink–drank**   I usually drink a cup of coffee in the morning. I drank a cup of coffee this morning. What did I do this morning? Did you drink a cup of coffee this morning? What do you usually drink in the morning? Do you drink the same thing every morning?

9. **drive–drove**   I usually drive my car to school. I drove my car to school this morning. What did I do this morning? Who has a car? Did you drive to school this morning?

10. **ride–rode**   Sometimes I ride the bus to school. I rode the bus yesterday morning. What did I do yesterday morning? Who rode the bus to school this morning?

11. **REVIEW:** I was late for class yesterday morning, so what did I do? What did I read yesterday? What did you read yesterday? Did you read a newspaper this morning? What did I drink this morning? What did you drink this morning? I have a car. Did I drive to school this morning? Did you? Did you ride the bus?

☐ EXERCISE 35. Sentence practice.
    Directions: Complete the sentences. Use the words in parentheses.

1. A: Why are you out of breath?

   B: I *(run)* _____ to class because I was late.

2. A: I *(ride)* _____ the bus to school yesterday. How did you get to

   school?

   B: I *(drive)* _____ my car.

3. A: Did you decide to change schools?

   B: I *(think)* _____ about it, but then I decided to stay here.

4. A: *(you, go)* _____ shopping yesterday?

   B: Yes. I *(buy)* _____ a new pair of shoes.

5. A: *(you, study)* _____ last night?

   B: No, I didn't. I was tired. I *(read)* _____ a magazine and then

   (go) _____ to bed early.

6. A: Do you like milk?

   B: No. I *(drink)* _____ milk when I *(be)* _____

   a child, but I don't like milk now.

7. A: Did you leave your dictionary at home?

   B: No. I *(bring)* _____ it to class with me.

8. Yesterday Yoko *(teach)* _____ us how to say "thank you" in

   Japanese. Kim *(teach)* _____ us how to say "I love you" in

   Korean.

9. A: Did you enjoy your fishing trip?

   B: I had a wonderful time! I *(catch)* _____ a lot of fish.

☐ EXERCISE 36. Let's talk: pairwork.

   Directions: Work with a partner. Take turns asking and answering questions about the past.

   Partner A: Make a complete question with the given verb. Use the simple past.
   Ask your partner the question.

   Partner B: Answer the question. Give both a short answer and a long answer.

   Example: drink
   PARTNER A: Did you drink a cup of coffee this morning?
   PARTNER B: Yes, I did. I drank a cup of coffee this morning. OR
   No, I didn't. I didn't drink a cup of coffee this morning.
   PARTNER A: Your turn now.

Partner A	Partner B
1. eat	1. sleep
2. buy	2. go
3. get up	3. talk to
4. have	4. walk
5. go	5. watch
6. study	6. listen to
7. drink	7. see
8. read	8. think about
9. drive	9. rain

□ **EXERCISE 37. Listening.**

Directions: Listen to the beginning of each sentence. Circle the correct completion(s). There may be more than one correct answer.

Example: He drank . . . . 　　bread　　(some tea)　　(water)

1. last week	a fish	happy
2. very fast	a house	to the store
3. books	the children	the newspaper
4. a story	yesterday	a horse
5. good	some food	a doctor
6. people	into town	home

□ **EXERCISE 38. Writing practice.**

Directions: Use the expressions in the list below to write sentences about yourself. When did you do these things *in the past?* Use the simple past tense and past time expressions (**yesterday, two days ago, last week,** etc.) in all of your sentences.

Example: go downtown with *(someone)*
Response: I went downtown with Marco two days ago.

1. arrive in *(this city)*
2. eat at a restaurant
3. buy *(something)*
4. have a cold
5. be in elementary school
6. drink a cup of tea
7. talk to *(someone)* on the phone
8. study arithmetic
9. read a newspaper
10. play (soccer, a pinball machine, etc.)
11. see *(someone or something)*
12. think about *(someone or something)*
13. be born

8-10 IRREGULAR VERBS (GROUP 3)

break – broke	*meet – met*	*sing – sang*
fly – flew	*pay – paid*	*speak – spoke*
hear – heard	*ring – rang*	*take – took*
leave – left	*send – sent*	*wake up – woke up*

☐ EXERCISE 39. Let's talk: class activity.

Directions: Practice using irregular verbs. Close your book for this activity.

Example: **break–broke**
TEACHER: break–broke. Sometimes a person breaks an arm or a leg.
 I broke my arm five years ago. What happened five years ago?
STUDENTS: (repeat) break–broke. You broke your arm.
TEACHER: (to Student A) Did you ever break a bone?
STUDENT A: Yes. I broke my leg ten years ago.

1. **fly–flew**   Sometimes I fly home in an airplane. I flew home in an airplane last month. What did I do last month? When did you fly to this city?

2. **hear–heard**   I hear birds singing every morning. I heard birds singing yesterday. What did I hear yesterday? What did you hear when you woke up this morning?

3. **pay–paid**   I pay the rent every month. I paid the rent last month. What did I do last month? Did you pay your rent last month?

4. **send–sent**   I send my mother a gift every year on her birthday. I sent my mother a gift last year on her birthday. What did I do last year? When did you send a gift to someone?

5. **leave–left**   I leave for school at 8:00 every morning. I left for school yesterday at 8:00 A.M. What did I do at 8:00 A.M. yesterday? What time did you leave for class this morning?

6. **meet–met**   I meet new people every week. Yesterday I met (. . .)'s friend. What did I do yesterday? Do you know (. . .)? When did you meet him/her?

7. **take–took**   I take my younger brother to the movies every month. I took my younger brother to the movies last month. What did I do last month? Who has a younger brother or sister? Where and when did you take him/her someplace?

8. **wake–woke**   I usually wake up at six. This morning I woke up at six-thirty. What time did I wake up this morning? What time did you wake up this morning?

9. **speak–spoke**   I speak to many students every day. Before class today, I spoke to (. . .). Who did I speak to? Who did you speak to before class today?

10. **ring–rang**   The phone in our apartment rings a lot. This morning it rang at six-thirty and woke me up. What happened at six-thirty this morning? Who had a telephone call this morning? What time did the phone ring?

11. **sing–sang**   I sing in the shower every morning. I sang in the shower yesterday. What did I do yesterday? Do you ever sing? When was the last time?

12. **break–broke**   Sometimes I break things. This morning I dropped a glass on the floor, and it broke. What happened this morning? When did you break something?

☐ EXERCISE 40. Sentence practice.
Directions: Complete the sentences. Use the correct form of the verbs in the list.

break	leave	ring	speak
fly	meet	send	take
hear	pay	sing	wake

1. A: What happened to your finger?

   B: I _____ it in a soccer game.

2. A: Who did you talk to at the director's office?

   B: I _____ to the secretary.

3. A: When did Jessica leave for Europe?

   B: She _____ for Europe five days ago.

4. A: Did you write Ted a letter?

   B: No, but I _____ him a postcard.

5. A: Do you know Meg Adams?

   B: Yes. I _____ her a couple of weeks ago.

6. A: Why did you call the police?

   B: Because I _____ a burglar!

7. A: Where did you go yesterday?

   B: I _____ the children to the zoo.

8. A: What time did you get up this morning?

   B: 6:15.

   A: Why did you get up so early?

   B: The telephone _____.

9. A: Did you enjoy the party?

   B: Yes, I had a good time. We _____ songs and danced. It was fun.

10. A: You look sleepy.

   B: I am. I _____ up before dawn this morning and couldn't get

   back to sleep.

11. A: A bird _____ into our apartment

   yesterday through an open window.

   B: Really? What did you do?

   A: I caught it and took it outside.

12. A: Did you give the painter a check?

   B: No. I _____ him in cash.

☐ **EXERCISE 41. Listening.**

   Directions: Listen to the story. Then read each sentence and circle the best answer.

   1. The man was at the doctor's office.   yes   no
   2. He took some medicine.   yes   no
   3. He was in bed for a short time.   yes   no
   4. The man spoke to the nurse.   yes   no
   5. He is feeling okay now.   yes   no

8-11 IRREGULAR VERBS (GROUP 4)

begin – began	*say – said*	*tell – told*
find – found	*sell – sold*	*tear – tore*
lose – lost	*steal – stole*	*wear – wore*
hang – hung		

☐ **EXERCISE 42. Let's talk: class activity.**

   Directions: Practice using irregular verbs. Close your book for this activity.

   Example: **begin–began**
   TEACHER: begin–began. Our class begins at (9:00) every day. Class began at (9:00
        this morning). When did class begin (this morning)?
   STUDENTS: *(repeat)* begin–began. Class began (this morning) at (9:00).

1. *lose–lost*   Sometimes I lose things. Yesterday I lost my keys. What did I lose yesterday?

2. *find–found*   Sometimes I lose things. And then I find them. Yesterday I lost my keys, but then I found them in my jacket pocket. What did I do yesterday?

3. *tear–tore*   If we make a mistake when we write a check, we tear the check up. Yesterday I made a mistake when I wrote a check, so I tore it up and wrote a new check. What did I do yesterday?

4. *sell–sold*   People sell things that they don't need anymore. (. . .) has a new bicycle, so he/she sold his/her old bicycle. What did (. . .) do?

5. *hang–hung*   I like to hang pictures on my walls. This morning I hung a new picture in my bedroom. What did I do this morning?

6. *tell–told*   The kindergarten teacher likes to tell stories to her students. Yesterday she told a story about a little red train. What did the teacher do yesterday?

7. *wear–wore*   I wear a sweater to class every evening. Last night I wore a jacket as well. What did I wear last night?

8. *steal–stole*   Thieves steal money and other valuables. Last month a thief stole my aunt's pearl necklace. What did a thief do last month?

9. *say–said*   People usually say "hello" when they answer a phone. When (. . .) answered his/her phone this morning, he/she said "hello." What did (. . .) do this morning?

☐ EXERCISE 43. Sentence practice.
   Directions: Complete the sentences with the given words.

begin	*say*	*tear*
find	*sell*	*tell*
hang	*steal*	*wear*
lose		

1. A: Did you go to the park yesterday?

   B: No. We stayed home because it _____ to rain.

   A: Oh, that's too bad.

2. A: Susie is in trouble.

   B: Why?

   A: She _____ a lie. Her mom and dad are upset.

   B: I'm sure she's sorry.

3. A: May I please have your homework?

   B: I don't have it. I _____ it.

   A: What?

   B: I can't find it anywhere.

4. A: Where's my coat?

   B: I _____ it up in the closet for you.

5. A: Where did you get that pretty shell?

   B: I _____ it on the beach.

   shells

6. A: Do you still have your bicycle?

   B: No. I _____ it because I needed some extra money.

7. A: It's hot in here.

   B: Excuse me? What did you say?

   A: I _____, "It's hot in here."

8. A: Why did you take the bus to work this morning? Why didn't you drive?

   B: Because somebody _____ my car last night.

   A: Did you call the police?

   B: Of course I did.

9. A: Did you wear your blue jeans to the job interview?

   B: Of course not! I _____ a suit.

10. A: I wrote the wrong amount on the check,

    so I had to write a new check.

    B: What did you do with the first check?

    A: I _____ it into pieces.

☐ **EXERCISE 44. Listening.**

Directions: Listen to the story. Then read each sentence and circle the best answer.

1. The woman lost her mother's ring.   yes   no

2. Someone stole the ring.   yes   no

3. Her dog found the ring in the garden.   yes   no

4. Her mother wore the ring for a while.   yes   no

5. The woman was happy at the end of the story.   yes   no

☐ **EXERCISE 45. Chapter review.**

Directions: You went to a birthday party last night. A friend is asking you questions about it. Complete the sentences with *did, was,* or *were.*

1. _____ you go with a friend?

2. _____ your friends at the party?

3. _____ the party fun?

4. _____ many people there?

5. _____ you have a good time?

6. _____ you eat a piece of birthday cake?

7. _____ everyone sing "Happy Birthday"?

8. _____ there a birthday cake?

9. _____ you hungry?

10. _____ you take a present?

☐ **EXERCISE 46. Chapter review.**

Directions: Complete the sentences with *was, were,* or *did.*

1. I _____*did*_____ not go to work yesterday. I _____*was_____ sick, so I stayed home from the office.

2. Tom _____ not in his office yesterday. He _____ not go to work.

3. A: _____ Mr. Chan in his office yesterday?

   B: Yes.

   A: _____ you see him about your problem?

   B: Yes. He answered all my questions. He _____ very helpful.

4. A: _____ you at the meeting yesterday?

   B: What meeting?

   A: _____ you forget about the meeting?

   B: I guess so. What meeting?

   A: The meeting with the president of the company about health insurance.

   B: Oh. Now I remember. No, I _____ not there. _____ you?

   A: Yes. I can tell you all about it.

   B: Thanks.

5. A: Where _____ you yesterday?

   B: I _____ at the zoo.

   A: _____ you enjoy it?

   B: Yes, but the weather _____ very hot. I tried to stay out of the sun. Most

   of the animals _____ in their houses or in the shade. The sun

   _____ too hot for them too. They _____ not want to be outside.

□ EXERCISE 47. Chapter review.
   Directions: Make questions and give short answers.

   1. A: _____*Do you live in an apartment?*_____

      B: _____*Yes, I do.*_____ (I live in an apartment.)

   2. A: _____*Do you have a roommate?*_____

      B: _____*No, I don't.*_____ (I don't have a roommate.)

3. A: _____

   B: _____ (I don't want a roommate.)

4. A: _____

   B: _____ (I had a roommate last year.)
      It didn't work out.

5. A: _____

   B: _____ (He was difficult to live with.)
   A: What did he do?
   B: He never picked up his dirty clothes. He never washed his dirty dishes. He
      was always late with his share of the rent.

6. A: _____

   B: _____ (I asked him to keep the apartment clean.)
      He always agreed, but he never did it.

7. A: _____

   B: _____ (I was glad when he left.)
      I like living alone.

□ EXERCISE 48. Class activity.

Directions: Walk around the room. Ask your classmates questions about the present
and the past. Change classmates with every topic.

Example: walk to school
SPEAKER A: Do you walk to school every day?
SPEAKER B: Yes, I do. OR No, I don't.
SPEAKER A: Did you walk to school this morning?
SPEAKER B: Yes, I did. I walked with a friend. OR No, I didn't.

1. go downtown
2. dream in color
3. talk to *(someone)* on the phone
4. come to grammar class on time
5. sing in the shower
6. eat at least two pieces of fresh fruit
7. think about your family
8. cook your own dinner

9. wear *(an article of clothing)*
10. laugh out loud at least two times
11. speak *(a language)*
12. go to *(a place in this city)*
13. read at least one book
14. go swimming
15. go shopping

□ **EXERCISE 49. Let's talk: game.**

Directions: Your teacher will say the simple form of a verb. Your team will give the past tense. Close your book for this activity.

Example:
TEACHER: Team A: come
 TEAM A: *(all together)* came
TEACHER: That's one point.

TEACHER: Team B: eat
 TEAM B: *(all together)* ate
TEACHER: That's one point.

1. fly	11. pay	21. leave
2. bring	12. hear	22. have
3. read	13. catch	23. pay
4. tell	14. find	24. meet
5. stand	15. sleep	25. sit
6. teach	16. think	26. take
7. drink	17. ride	27. ring
8. wear	18. break	28. write
9. buy	19. say	29. sing
10. speak	20. get	30. wake up

□ **EXERCISE 50. Chapter review: error analysis.**

Directions: Correct the errors.

1. Someone stealed my bicycle two day ago.

2. Did you went to the party yesterday weekend?

3. I hear a really interesting story yesterday.

4. The teacher not ready for class yesterday.

5. Did came Joe to work last week?

6. Yesterday night I staied home and working on my science project.

7. Several students wasn't on time for the final exam yesterday.

8. Your fax came before ten minutes. Did you got it?

9. Did you all your friends to your graduation party invite?

10. I sleeped too late this morning and was missed the bus.

11. The market no have any bananas yesterday. I get there too late.

12. Was you nervous about your test the last week?

13. I didn't saw you at the party. Did you be there?

☐ EXERCISE 51. Review.

Directions: Think about the years your grandparents grew up in. What kinds of things did they do? What kinds of things didn't they do? Write sentences. Work with a partner or in small groups.

Example: My grandparents didn't use computers.
My grandfather walked to work.

APPENDIX
Irregular Verbs

SIMPLE FORM	SIMPLE PAST	SIMPLE FORM	SIMPLE PAST
be	was, were	keep	kept
become	became	know	knew
begin	began	leave	left
bend	bent	lend	lent
bite	bit	lose	lost
blow	blew	make	made
break	broke	meet	met
bring	brought	pay	paid
build	built	put	put
buy	bought	read	read
catch	caught	ride	rode
choose	chose	ring	rang
come	came	run	ran
cost	cost	say	said
cut	cut	see	saw
do	did	sell	sold
draw	drew	send	sent
drink	drank	shake	shook
drive	drove	shut	shut
eat	ate	sing	sang
fall	fell	sit	sat
feed	fed	sleep	slept
feel	felt	speak	spoke
fight	fought	spend	spent
find	found	stand	stood
fly	flew	steal	stole
forget	forgot	swim	swam
get	got	take	took
give	gave	teach	taught
go	went	tear	tore
grow	grew	tell	told
hang	hung	think	thought
have	had	throw	threw
hear	heard	understand	understood
hide	hid	wake up	woke up
hit	hit	wear	wore
hold	held	win	won
hurt	hurt	write	wrote

Listening Script

Chapter 1: USING *BE*

EXERCISE 2, p. 2.

Paulo is a student from Brazil. Marie is a student from France. They're in the classroom. Today is an exciting day. It's the first day of school, but they aren't nervous. They're happy to be here. Mrs. Brown is the teacher. She isn't in the classroom right now. She's late today.

EXERCISE 8, p. 6.

1. Butterflies are insects.
2. English is a country.
3. Spring is a season.
4. Canada is a city.
5. Japan is a language.
6. Roses are flowers.
7. Rabbits are machines.
8. Russian and Arabic are languages.
9. Cows are animals.

EXERCISE 13, p. 9.

1. I like my teachers. They're very nice.
2. I am at school. I'm in the classroom.
3. Yuri is not here. He's late.
4. I know you. You're a teacher.
5. I know Susan. I'm her friend.
6. Ali and I are friends. We're in the same class.
7. My sister has two children. They're young.
8. Los Angeles is a city. It's very big.
9. Anna is from Russia. She's very friendly.
10. I like soccer. It's fun.

EXERCISE 14, p. 9.

SPEAKER A: Hello. My name is Mrs. Brown. I'm the new teacher.
SPEAKER B: Hi. My name is Paulo, and this is Marie. We're in your class.
SPEAKER A: It's nice to meet you.
SPEAKER B: We're happy to meet you too.
SPEAKER A: It's time for class. Please take a seat.

EXERCISE 29, p. 22.

1. Grammar's easy.
2. My name's John.
3. My books're on the table.
4. My brother's 21 years old.
5. The weather's cold today.
6. The windows're open.
7. My money's in my wallet.
8. Mr. Smith's a teacher.
9. Mrs. Lee's at home now.
10. The sun's bright today.
11. Tom's at home right now.
12. My roommates're from Chicago.
13. My sister's a student in high school.

EXERCISE 30, p. 22.

1. The test's easy.
2. My notebook is on the table.
3. My notebooks are on the table.
4. Sue's a student.
5. The weather is warm today.
6. The windows're open.
7. My parents're from Cuba.
8. My cousins are from Cuba too.
9. My book's on my desk.
10. The teachers're in class.

Chapter 2: USING *BE* AND *HAVE*

EXERCISE 1, p. 24.

1. Are England and Canada cities?
2. Is winter a season?
3. Are bananas blue?
4. Is the weather very cold today?
5. Are airplanes slow?
6. Is a carrot a machine?
7. Are diamonds free?
8. Is the earth round?
9. Are big cities quiet?

EXERCISE 12, p. 32.
1. The boots have zippers.
2. Anna has a raincoat.
3. Her raincoat has buttons.
4. Her sweater has long sleeves.
5. She has earrings on her ears.
6. The earrings have diamonds.
7. You have long pants.
8. We have warm coats.

EXERCISE 22, p. 39.
1. This is my grammar book.
2. That is your grammar book.
3. That's your wallet.
4. This's her purse.
5. Is that your umbrella?
6. This's not my umbrella.
7. Is this your ring?
8. Yes, that's my ring.
9. This isn't my homework.
10. That's their car.

Chapter 3: USING THE SIMPLE PRESENT

EXERCISE 2, p. 55.
1. I wake up early every day. → wake
2. My brother wakes up late.
3. He gets up at 11:00.
4. I go to school at 8:00.
5. My mother does exercises every morning.
6. My little sister watches TV in the morning.
7. I take the bus to school.
8. My brother takes the bus to school.
9. My friends take the bus too.
10. We talk about our day.

EXERCISE 8, p. 59.
1. I go to work every morning. → morning
2. I celebrate my birthday every year.
3. Our son is two years old.
4. I use my computer every day.
5. Bob uses his computer five days a week.
6. I eat three times a day.
7. Anna listens to the radio every night.
8. I visit my uncle every month.

EXERCISE 13, p. 62.
1. Mrs. Miller teaches English on Saturdays. → teaches
2. Mr. and Mrs. Smith teach English in the evenings.
3. Doug fixes cars.
4. His son fixes cars too.
5. Carlos and Chris watch DVDs on weekends.
6. Their daughter watches videos.
7. I brush my hair every morning.
8. Jimmy seldom brushes his hair.

9. The Johnsons wash their car every weekend.
10. Susan rarely washes her car.

EXERCISE 18, p. 65.
Marco is a student. He has an unusual schedule. All of his classes are at night. His first class is at 6:00 P.M. every day. He has a break from 7:30 to 8:00. Then he has classes from 8:00 to 10:00.

He leaves school and goes home at 10:00. After he has dinner, he watches TV. Then he does his homework from midnight to 3:00 or 4:00 in the morning.

Marco has his own computer at home. When he finishes his homework, he usually goes on the Internet. He usually stays at his computer until the sun comes up. Then he does a few exercises, has breakfast, and goes to bed. He sleeps all day. Marco thinks his schedule is great, but his friends think it is strange.

Chapter 4: USING THE PRESENT PROGRESSIVE

EXERCISE 7, p. 96.
1. Tony is sitting in the cafeteria.
2. He is sitting alone.
3. He is wearing a hat.
4. He is eating lunch.
5. He is reading his grammar book.
6. He is looking at his computer.
7. He is studying hard.
8. He is smiling.
9. He is listening to the radio.
10. He is waving to his friends.

EXERCISE 21, p. 107.
1. I write in my grammar book . . . .
2. I am writing in my grammar book . . . .
3. It is raining outside . . . .
4. It doesn't rain . . . .
5. My cell phone rings . . . .
6. My cell phone isn't ringing . . . .
7. My friends and I listen to music in the car . . . .
8. We're not listening to music . . . .

EXERCISE 25, p. 110.
1. A: Does Tom have a black hat?
   B: Yes.
   A: Does he wear it every day?
   B: No.
   A: Is he wearing it right now?
   B: I don't know. Why do you care about Tom's hat?
   A: I found a hat in my apartment. Someone left it there. I think that it belongs to Tom.
2. A: Do animals dream?
   B: I don't know. I suppose so. Animals aren't very different from human beings in lots of ways.

A: Look at my dog. She is sleeping. Her eyes are closed. At the same time, she is barking and moving her head and her front legs. I am sure that she is dreaming right now. I'm sure that animals dream.

EXERCISE 26, p. 111.

SPEAKER A: What are you doing? Are you working on your English paper?

SPEAKER B: No, I'm not. I'm writing an e-mail to my sister.

SPEAKER A: Do you write to her often?

SPEAKER B: Yes, but I don't write a lot of e-mails to anyone else.

SPEAKER A: Does she write to you often?

SPEAKER B: Yes. I get an e-mail from her several times a week. How about you? Do you get a lot of e-mails?

SPEAKER A: Yes. I like to send e-mails to friends all over the world.

Chapter 5: TALKING ABOUT THE PRESENT

EXERCISE 1, p. 121.

1. What time is it?
2. What month is it?
3. What day is it today?
4. What year is it?
5. What's the date today?

EXERCISE 4, p. 124.

1. My birthday is in June. I was born on June 24. I have class every day at 1:00. Who am I?
2. I have class at 7:00. I go to class in the morning. I was born in 1986. Who am I?
3. I have class in the morning. I was born in July. I was born in 1990. Who am I?
4. I was born in 1989. My birthday is July 7. I go to class at night. Who am I?

EXERCISE 12, p. 130.

1. There're ten students in the classroom.
2. There's a new teacher today.
3. There're two teachers outside.
4. There's a book on the floor.
5. There's some information on the blackboard.
6. There're several papers in the wastepaper basket.
7. There're two coffee cups on the teacher's desk.
8. There's a lot of homework for tomorrow.

EXERCISE 23, p. 138.

1. There are trees behind the train.
2. A bird is under the picnic table.
3. There are butterflies in the air.
4. There is a fishing pole on top of the table.
5. There is a knife on top of the table.
6. A boat is in the water.
7. The bridge is below the water.
8. There are clouds above the hills.
9. There are flowers beside the river.
10. There are flowers next to the river.
11. The guitar is under the table.
12. One bike is under the tree.
13. The fish is on the grass.
14. The table is between the tree and the river.
15. The flowers are near the water.

EXERCISE 31, p. 145.

1. A: Where do you want to go for dinner tonight?
   B: Rossini's Restaurant.
2. A: What time do you want to go to the airport?
   B: Around five. My plane leaves at seven.
3. A: Jean doesn't want to go to the baseball game.
   B: Why not?
   A: Because she needs to study for a test.
4. A: I'm getting tired. I want to take a break for a few minutes.
   B: Okay. Let's take a break. We can finish the work later.
5. A: We don't need to come to class on Friday.
   B: Why not?
   A: It's a holiday.
6. A: Peter wants to go back to his apartment.
   B: Why?
   A: Because he wants to change his clothes before he goes to the party.
7. A: Where do you want to go for your vacation?
   B: I want to visit Niagara Falls, Quebec, and Montreal.
8. A: May I see your dictionary? I need to look up a word.
   B: Of course. Here it is.
   A: Thanks.
9. A: Do you want to go with us to the park?
   B: Sure. Thanks. I need to get some exercise.

EXERCISE 32, p. 147.

1. Tony'd like a cup of coffee.
2. He'd like some sugar in his coffee.
3. Ahmed and Anita'd like some coffee too.
4. They'd like some sugar in their coffee too.
5. A: Would you like a cup of coffee? ("Would you" can't be contracted in short answers or questions.)
   B: Yes, I would. Thank you.
6. I'd like to thank you for your kindness and hospitality.
7. My friends'd like to thank you too.
8. A: Would Robert like to ride with us?
   B: Yes, he would.

EXERCISE 34, p. 148.

1. I'd like a hamburger for dinner.
2. We like to eat in fast-food restaurants.
3. Bob'd like to go to the gym now.
4. He likes to exercise after work.
5. The teacher'd like to speak with you.
6. I think the teacher likes you.
7. We like to ride our bikes on weekends.
8. Bill and Sue like classical music.
9. They'd like to go to a concert next week.
10. I think I'd like to go with them.

Chapter 6: NOUNS AND PRONOUNS

EXERCISE 12, p. 166.

1. Sara knows Joe. She knows him ("knows 'im") very well.
2. Where does Shelley live? Do you have her ("have-er") address?
3. There's Sam. Let's go talk to him ("im").
4. There's Bill and Julie. Let's go talk to them ("em").
5. The teacher is speaking with Lisa because she doesn't have her ("have-er") homework.
6. I need to see our airline tickets. Do you have them ("have-em")?

EXERCISE 13, p. 167.

1. A: Yoko and I are ("I-er") going downtown this afternoon. Do you want to ("wanna") come with us?
   B: I don't think so, but thanks anyway. Chris and I are going to the library. We need to study for our test.
2. A: Hi, Ann. How do you like your new apartment?
   B: It's very nice.
   A: Do you have a roommate?
   B: Yes. Maria Hall is my roommate. Do you know her ("know-er")? She's from Miami.
   A: No, I don't know her ("know-er"). Do you get along with her?
   B: Yes, we enjoy living together. You must visit us sometime. Maybe you can come over for dinner soon.
   A: Thanks. I'd like that.
3. A: Do George and Mike come over to your house often?
   B: Yes, they do. I invite them to my house often. We like to play cards.
   A: Who usually wins your card games?
   B: Mike. He's a really good card player. We can't beat him.

EXERCISE 15, p. 170.

GROUP A. Final *-s* is pronounced /z/ after voiced sounds.

1. taxicabs	5. rooms	9. trees
2. beds	6. coins	10. cities
3. dogs	7. years	11. boys
4. balls	8. lives	12. days

GROUP B. Final *-s* is pronounced /s/ after voiceless sounds.

13. books	16. groups
14. desks	17. cats
15. cups	18. students

GROUP C. Final *-es* is pronounced /əz/.

- after "s" sounds:
  - 19. classes
  - 20. glasses
  - 21. horses
  - 22. places
  - 23. sentences
- after "z" sounds:
  - 24. sizes
  - 25. exercises
  - 26. noises
- after "sh" sounds:
  - 27. dishes
  - 28. bushes
- after "ch" sounds:
  - 29. matches
  - 30. sandwiches
- after "ge/dge" sounds:
  - 31. pages
  - 32. oranges
  - 33. bridges

EXERCISE 16, p. 171.

1. toys	6. boxes
2. table	7. package
3. face	8. chairs
4. hats	9. edge
5. offices	10. tops

EXERCISE 17, p. 172.

1. The desks in the classroom are new. → desks
2. I like to visit new places.
3. Donna wants a sandwich for lunch.
4. The teacher is correcting sentences with a red pen.
5. This apple is delicious.
6. The students are finishing a writing exercise in class.
7. I need two pieces of paper.
8. Roses are beautiful flowers.
9. Your rose bush is beautiful.
10. The college has many scholarships for students.

Chapter 7: COUNT AND NONCOUNT NOUNS

EXERCISE 6, p. 184.

1. I live in an apartment. → an
2. It's a small apartment.
3. My English class lasts an hour.

4. It's an interesting class.
5. We have a new teacher.
6. My mother has an office downtown.
7. It's an insurance office.
8. My father is a nurse.
9. He works at a hospital.
10. He has a difficult job.

EXERCISE 31, p. 204.

1. Vegetables have vitamins. → general
2. Cats make nice pets.
3. The teacher is absent.
4. I love bananas.
5. New cars are expensive.
6. I need the keys to the car.
7. Are the computers in your office working?
8. Let's feed the ducks at the park.

EXERCISE 32, p. 205.

1. A: Do you have a pen?
   B: There's one on the counter in the kitchen.
2. A: Where are the keys to the car?
   B: I'm not sure, but I have a set. You can use mine.
3. A: Shh. I hear a noise.
   B: It's just a bird outside, probably a woodpecker. Don't worry.
4. A: John Jones teaches at the university.
   B: I know. He's an English professor.
   A: He's also the head of the department.
5. A: Hurry! We're late.
   B: No, we're not. It's five o'clock, and we have an hour.
   A: No, it isn't. It's six! Look at the clock.
   B: Oh, my. I need a new battery in my watch.

Chapter 8: EXPRESSING PAST TIME, PART 1

EXERCISE 5, p. 215.

1. I wasn't at home last night. → wasn't
2. I was at the library.
3. Our teacher was sick yesterday.
4. He wasn't at school.
5. Many students were absent.
6. They weren't at school for several days.
7. There was a substitute teacher.
8. She was very patient and kind.
9. My friends and I weren't nervous on the first day of school.
10. We were very relaxed.

EXERCISE 14, p. 224.

1. Mary played the piano for the class. → played
2. She plays very well.
3. The students watched an interesting movie.

4. They enjoyed it a lot.
5. They often watch movies together.
6. The class asked the teacher many questions.
7. The teacher answered their questions clearly.
8. The students listened very carefully.
9. They like their class.
10. The class works very hard.

EXERCISE 18, p. 226.

PART I.

1. What day was it two days ago?
2. What day was it five days ago?
3. What day was it yesterday?
4. What month was it last month?
5. What year was it ten years ago?
6. What year was it last year?
7. What year was it one year ago?

PART II.

8. What time was it one hour ago?
9. What time was it five minutes ago?
10. What time was it one minute ago?

EXERCISE 22, p. 230.

1. I ate . . . .
2. We sat . . . .
3. They came . . . .
4. She had . . . .
5. He got . . . .
6. I stood . . . .

EXERCISE 30, p. 235.

1. Did we do well on the test?
2. Did you finish the assignment?
3. Did it make sense?
4. Did I answer your question?
5. Did they need more help?
6. Did he understand the homework?
7. Did I explain the project?
8. Did they complete the project?
9. Did you do well?
10. Did she pass the class?

EXERCISE 33, p. 237.

PART I.

1. Did you ("did-juh") read the paper this morning?
2. A: Tom called.
   B: Did he ("dih-de") leave a message?
3. A: Sara called.
   B: Did she ("dih-she") leave a message?
4. Did it ("dih-dit") rain yesterday?
5. A: The children are watching TV.
   B: Did they ("dih-they") finish their homework?
6. I can't find my notebook. Did I ("dih-di") leave it on your desk?

PART II.

1. Did you ("did-juh") finish the homework assignment?

2. Did it ("dih-dit") take a long time?
3. Did you ("dih-juh") hear my question?
4. Did they ("dih-they") hear my question?
5. Did I ("dih-di") speak loud enough?
6. Did he ("dih-de") understand the information?
7. Did she ("dih-she") understand the information?
8. Did you ("dih-juh") want more help?
9. Did I ("dih-di") explain it okay?
10. Did he ("dih-de") do a good job?

EXERCISE 37, p. 241.

1. She caught . . . .   4. I rode . . . .
2. They drove . . . .   5. He bought . . . .
3. We read . . . .   6. We ran . . . .

EXERCISE 41, p. 244.

    I woke up with a headache this morning. I took some medicine and went back to bed. I slept all day. The phone rang. I heard it, but I was very tired. I didn't answer it. I listened to the answering machine. It was the doctor's office. The nurse said I missed my appointment. Now my headache is really bad!

EXERCISE 44, p. 247.

    My mother called me early this morning. She had wonderful news for me. She had my wedding ring. I lost it many years ago. I thought someone stole it, but she told me, "No, it didn't happen that way." She told me she was outside in her garden recently with her dog. The dog brought her something. She thought it was money. Then she saw it was my ring. She put it on her finger and wore it. She didn't want to lose it again. I was so happy. I hung up the phone and began to laugh and cry at the same time.

AUDIO CD TRACKING SCRIPT

CD 1	TRACK	EXERCISE
Introduction	1	
Chapter 1	2	Exercise 2, p. 2
	3	Exercise 8, p. 6
	4	Exercise 13, p. 9
	5	Exercise 14, p. 9
	6	Exercise 29, p. 22
	7	Exercise 30, p. 22
Chapter 2	8	Exercise 1, p. 24
	9	Exercise 12, p. 32
	10	Exercise 22, p. 39
Chapter 3	11	Exercise 2, p. 55
	12	Exercise 8, p. 59
	13	Exercise 13, p. 62
	14	Exercise 18, p. 65
Chapter 4	15	Exercise 7, p. 96
	16	Exercise 21, p. 107
	17	Exercise 25, p. 110
	18	Exercise 26, p. 111
Chapter 5	19	Exercise 1, p. 121
	20	Exercise 4, p. 124
	21	Exercise 12, p. 130
	22	Exercise 23, p. 138
	23	Exercise 31, p. 145
	24	Exercise 32, p. 147
	25	Exercise 34, p. 148
Chapter 6	26	Exercise 12, p. 166
	27	Exercise 13, p. 167
	28	Exercise 15, p. 170
	29	Exercise 16, p. 171
	30	Exercise 17, p. 172
Chapter 7	31	Exercise 6, p. 184
	32	Exercise 31, p. 204
	33	Exercise 32, p. 205
Chapter 8	34	Exercise 5, p. 215
	35	Exercise 14, p. 224
	36	Exercise 18, p. 226
	37	Exercise 22, p. 230
	38	Exercise 30, p. 235
	39	Exercise 33, p. 237
	40	Exercise 37, p. 241
	41	Exercise 41, p. 244
	42	Exercise 44, p. 247

Index

A/an, 2, 4, 183 *(Look on pages 2, 4, and 183.)*	The numbers following the words listed in the index refer to page numbers in the text.
Consonants, 2*fn*. *(Look at the footnote on page 2.)*	The letters *fn*. mean "footnote." Footnotes are at the bottom of a chart or the bottom of a page.